*I dedicate this book to my beloved adoptive mother, June Clement;
to my wise and supporting adoptive father, Richard Clement;
and to my dear wife, Amy.*

Contents

Prologue

Who am I? I believe I am the son of a Korean woman and an American military man. I look like I am of mixed race. My orphanage papers say that I am, but the identity of my father and mother are lost.

How old am I? I believe I was born in 1951. My orphanage papers say 1952 but a little sleuthing has revealed that a year was subtracted from my age at the orphanage, perhaps to make me more adoptable. Actually, neither the orphanage nor I know my true age.

But all this is not important. What is important is that I survived. I survived because there were people who loved me and protected me at certain critical times of my life.

The following story is not fiction. The purpose of this book is to bring to the forefront some very sensitive topics. Topics such as biracial children, adoption and abandonment are laced throughout the text in hopes of illuminating these subjects. But, as is the nature of illumination, shadows will be cast. And, if humor is used, it is not used to demean the message; it is there to help sweeten the bitter pill of reality.

As in most wars, the Korean War left many abandoned children. Some were inadvertently separated from their birth parents due to the overwhelming confusion of the actual fighting. Some were intentionally left on street corners, police stations and orphanages by parents or relatives unable to care for them properly.

Many of the abandoned children were left to fend for themselves because they were biracial offspring of Korean women and foreign military men. Many societies do not accept biracial children because it is believed these children contaminate the race. This was true of Korean society in the Korean War period.

The mothers of some abandoned children were rape victims; some were left by their serviceman lovers once their pregnancy was discovered. Still others found themselves alone when their serviceman husbands or lovers were killed in action. If one does not know the circumstances of a woman abandoning a child in the tumultuous times of war it is wrong to render judgment.

The Unforgotten War

In June 1950, during a period of heightened "Cold War" tension, fighting broke out between North and South Korea. Fighting raged across the entire length of the two Koreas for three years, leaving both North and South Korea devastated. Most of the killed and wounded were Korean soldiers and civilians, 10% of the prewar population. This horrendous loss occurred in a country the size of two U.S. states combined, New York and Pennsylvania, with a population of 30,000,000. In the end, a truce left the border between the two countries almost unchanged. The same cannot be said of the people caught in the war.

In America the Korean War has often been characterized as the *forgotten war*. The **forgotten** war? How does one forget a war? How does one forget cheap death and massive destruction? How does one forget the ear-splitting sound of an exploding shell which shakes the very bones and soul of humans near the blast; especially an impressionable child who is in the process of figuring out life itself? It has been well over forty years since I was a child in Korea during the war. It was yesterday.

There is a saying that time heals all. Whoever says that has never been in a war, certainly not as a child. I still have nightmares about experiences in the war that occurred when I was only one or two. They say one does not remember things that happened earlier than the age of three. I remember.

The sky is dark, there are many clouds from previous cannon shell explosions lingering in the air, blanketing the sky. A distant whistling noise becomes more and more clearly audible until there is no doubt what the sound is. An explosion from another shell lights up the smoky sky in a flash resembling a lightning strike followed by an earth-shattering, body-blasting, bone-crushing, sound-deafening BOOOOM!!!!!!!!!!!!!!!

I see an image of two military-issue rifles leaning up against a wall. This image flickers on and off like a strobe light as the explosion subsides. There are sounds of people crying and wailing, at first

1

very faint, growing in volume until their cries are as deafening as the explosion itself. I am so small I am being carried on someone's back. We are in flight, from where to where I do not know. There are Korean soldiers, American soldiers, Korean civilians, children running every which way. And I see the aftermath of battle: body parts…a leg, an arm, people being carried, people being dragged, people rushing everywhere. Someone grabs me by the arm and turns my head from the horror. But I want to see. In utter wonder I try to see.

I still have a distinct recollection of the smell of the smoke from the explosions. I have a vivid memory of the huge tires on the trucks that transported the soldiers. I also remember the mud. War is not conducted under sanitary conditions.

I recall lying in a bed at night hearing the sound of people yelling and crying outside in the busy streets, of explosions, of siren alarms to warn people of a coming air attack. Sometimes the warning was sufficient. When the sirens sounded all night lights were turned off so that we would not be easy targets for the enemy. I remember standing up and watching the flashes of light from explosions through the window.

This was my life. Isn't this the way everyone lives? Bombs and cannon shells fall from the sky on all people and children everywhere…don't they? This was not a unique catastrophe, an oddity, a chance occurrence, or an event that someday will end. This was a way of life. The war monster was forever present. It was in the very air we breathed. It was in the dark skies above. It was in the earth we walked upon.

You could look across ruined buildings and perceive an invisible rage that swept across the land. The earth shook. It was so loud, like a storm, shifting with the wind. The noise would come from one direction, then another. People were afraid the war storm would shift, without warning, in their direction and envelop them. If that happened there was only one thing you could do…run!

What am I to make of these memories? I probably was born and lived for the first two or three years of my life near the border between North and South Korea, the site of the most prolonged fighting. Perhaps my mother was a North Korean swept south in the ebb and flow of battle. My place of birth is unknown. My early home must have been wherever there was not fighting at the time. I remember being on the move. I remember the awful noise, the fear, the cold and the mud.

Korean Family

I lived with my mother until I was four or five. My mother was a tiny person. I grew to be a 6′ 1″ man so I was not a small child. I must have seemed gigantic to my mother.

When I was perhaps three, I remember an American military man, perhaps my father, coming to take my mother out on the town and leaving me at home in our apartment. He was always in uniform. We lived in a city and I was kept inside most of the time because my mother was unwed and I was *half-and-half*, half American and half Asian. Half-and-half children were a disgrace in Korea.

When I was old enough to walk behind the military man who visited my mother, he took me to the mountains. The mountains were very steep. I would follow behind him on a little dirt trail that meandered between poverty-stricken shacks. Once I stopped to stare. Out from a rundown shack a group of little children came to look at me. I was much more fortunate than they because I was well-fed and had adequate clothes and shoes. The other children ranged in size from shorter than me to twice my height and had no shoes or socks. They wore rags and were very skinny and dirty. I just stood and looked at them as they looked back at me. The military man came back down the path and asked, "What are you doing?" smiling curiously. He took my hand and led me onward, swinging me around the back of his neck so I rode from this higher view. We could travel much more quickly in this fashion.

Our destination was my grandmother's, who lived way up in the mountains. There were many other relatives living there. Nearby was a well with a little roof over it and a hand-crank pulley connected to a rope and bucket to draw water from far below the earth's surface. Though my grandmother's home was fairly small, it was very pleasant visiting there because it was more peaceful in the mountains than in the busy, loud town. Also, I was afforded a lot of attention there. The military man showed me how to take a stick with a string tied to it and anchor it into the ground. At the free end of the string, he tied a flying grasshopper by the leg. When the grasshopper tried to fly it could only fly around in circles, tethered to the stick. He grabbed my leg and said with a smile, "How would you like me to tie your leg like this and swing you around?" His teasing is a warm memory.

Just as I had been hidden in town, I was also kept mostly in seclusion in this mountain retreat. I did have company though. I awoke one night and looked across the floor of the room. It was covered with people, perhaps relatives, who were sleeping on the floor with what looked like mosquito netting over their heads. I crawled around inspecting everyone before going back to sleep.

One sunny day a little boy who was two or three years older than I decided he wanted to get a drink of water from the well. At the time, I was too young to know exactly what he was doing and why. He let the bucket down into the well to fill it with water. He was strong enough to turn the manual crank to lift the full bucket of water to where we stood, grab the handle, and let go of the crank. He grabbed the handle with both hands, but did not have the strength to lift the bucket up onto the well ledge. He struggled in frustration to no avail. He would not let go of the heavy bucket. His face was bright red and then, without warning, the bucket plummeted to the bottom of the well with him still grasping it tightly. His cries were heard but it was too late. Bigger people came running but the boy had fallen to his death at the bottom of the well. With the help of others a strong young man tied a rope to his waist and was lowered into the well to retrieve the body. It was a sad day for everyone; people cried in grief. I did not cry. I had seen people die before.

Street Life in Seoul

Life for me, in its more or less protected and supervised existence, was about to change drastically. One morning my mother dressed me in a heavy coat and a hat. We walked with another lady into the busy streets. We walked for a very long time; I was growing weary. We were on a street corner when she kneeled down and gave me a hug and kiss. She buttoned my coat as a loving mother would to ensure the warmth and safety of her beloved child. As she stood up she instructed me to look down the street and not turn around. My mother and the other lady then walked in the opposite direction as I stood for who knows how long looking down the road filled with people going about their business. When I finally turned around I was alone. I began to walk. I walked and walked and walked...alone.

I ended up in a desolate area of the city. A group of street kids came running toward me, surrounded me and in no time stole my coat, shoes, socks and hat. They pushed me down and were gone as fast as they had appeared. This made me cry. I began to walk again. Another group of street kids approached me. The smaller ones ridiculed me and pushed and hit me. One of the older boys in this group stopped them and stuck up for me. Lucky for me he had control over this small gang of kids. The rest of the kids changed their attitude. In spite of the fact that I was obviously a biracial "tuki" and they were pure Korean, they adopted me.

The Korean word *tuki* deserves some explanation. It means "foreign devil" and it is not a lighthearted epithet. The Korean people, like many Asiatic people, think of foreigners as devils not to be trusted. As a child in Korea I learned to think of myself as literally a devil. I was not entitled to an education, a job or the prospect of marrying a pure Korean woman. I was **taboo**. This condition in Korea at the time was impossible to eradicate.

I lived on the streets for who knows how long between the ages of four and six. My new friends taught me how to survive, how to beg, borrow and steal. They taught me how a small group of little individuals could work as an organized team to overpower grownups and get what was needed to survive the harsh street life of Korea in the unsettled time that followed the war. We were what other Koreans called "dust of the streets."

The U.S. military used long, half-inch wide strips of metal to secure cargo when it was shipped overseas. We found these strips, which we called "bandits," by foraging in military waste dumps. We would bend the strips back and forth until they snapped free, and with the smaller portion, perhaps no longer than 4-6 inches in length, I learned how to sharpen one end into a knife. Scraping it against a stone, building, or concrete would soon transform it into a sharp dagger. Then we'd find string or paper to wrap around the handle and spit on it until the handle felt comfortable to hold. It was important to have more than one weapon because in a street fight you could become separated from your knife and another had to be readily available. By making slits in our pants we could wear these hidden; we used them for self-protection.

Life on the streets was very harsh, a matter of survival. We were a small group of miniature survivalists. We ate anything we could find including garbage, and I soon contracted worms. We'd beg anyone we could for anything they would give us. Most of the time our requests were ignored. People would try to get away from us as quickly as possible. Once a soldier gave one of the older kids a piece of gum. The boy split it up into many pieces to share with the rest of us. He then tore the wrapper into many pieces so we could put it into our mouths with the gum to increase the bulk of our little pieces of gum. It reminds me of the story of Jesus splitting the loaves of bread amongst the crowd of followers so as to feed everyone.

Our group developed another method of feeding ourselves. We would find an alley on the back side of a restaurant. There we sometimes found discarded food, mostly uncooked and spoiled, always cold. One day we were looking down an alley when a restaurant shutter was lowered. A rope was connected to it on both sides so that the shutter became a kind of table. The store employee, perhaps the restaurant owner, placed a large bowl of hot food on the surface for a very old man to eat. The food was both liquid and solid. The older boys in our group, who were stronger and faster, picked up stones and anything else they could throw and started yelling and tormenting the old man. They showered him with missiles. He kept eating but finally he got up and chased the taunting boys. When he was far enough away from the food, two others ran up and stole the whole bowl.

It is very difficult to run with a hot bowl half-filled with hot liquid. The boys were smiling and running at the same time with liquid spilling everywhere. One boy scooped up some food in mid-run with his free hand and stuffed it into his mouth. I was the smallest in our group and was still learning to "get with the program." I did not run away and the old man grabbed me by my arm and started yelling and violently shaking me. He lifted me part-way off the ground and shook me so violently that my head spun. Some of the bigger kids in my gang ran up to him and began to hit and kick him until he let me go. Two of the kids got on each side of me and ran with me. We made our getaway. In a place of safety we ate in silence until the food was gone. After that we laid around and bragged of the great heist. One storyteller mimicked how I looked as the old man was shaking me. We laughed and laughed until tears came down our faces, but my arm and shoulder hurt for a long time.

When our restaurant alley foraging didn't feed us, we begged. I remember standing in front of a seafood vendor's cart with an urchin friend casting longing looks at the food on display. The vendor took pity on us and gave us each a conical seashell which we promptly sucked dry. Another time I chanced on a small boy picking maggots out of a piece of discarded meat. I joined him in grabbing and eating the squirming maggots until an older boy warned us that maggots were "bad bugs." This reflects a discriminating taste because beetles, ants and other kinds of bugs are regularly eaten in some societies. When you are hungry you don't always observe the niceties. While on the streets I ate mice, snails, salamanders, lizards, frogs, slugs, roots, grass, bark, dogs and cats, and every kind of fish we could catch.

As a result of the war, most Korean people were terribly impoverished during the period I was on the street. The only toy I can recall seeing a Korean boy play with was a bicycle wheel without a tire. He was rolling the wheel down an alley using a stick. He was with his mother, who took a very dim view of me and hastened her prized son away as fast as she could. In addition to being a *tuki* I must have looked like a scarecrow with my dirty rags and shoeless feet.

We always kept a wary eye out for Korean police and soldiers. They sometimes conducted "sweeps" to catch street gangs and lock them up. Since I was biracial, I had to be particularly careful. People like me had a way of disappearing when caught, forever. This was no secret in Korea.

We never led a settled existence while on the streets. Every night we searched for a safe place to sleep. We huddled into a tight pack to conserve body heat. Korea is not tropical and the nights can be extremely cold in winter. Freezing temperatures and snow are not uncommon so staying warm was not easy. We took shelter under bridges, inside culverts and in bombed buildings. Large rats were an ever-present menace and made some places unusable since the rat population was life-threatening even for five-year-olds. Infants would have been easy prey for rats in some places. Public buildings such as train stations were off limits to street children. We were literally black with dirt, dressed in rags, smelled badly and had a well-earned reputation for stealing. Entering a public building, much less sleeping in one, was an invitation for retaliation from the decent public. The Korean people are not a cruel people, but in the 1950s most of them survived by only a narrow margin and family had to come first. Outsiders, particularly bastard children (or worse, biracial bastard children) were beyond the pale.

Disease was ever present. Cholera in particular took a heavy toll on the war-weakened Korean people and fell hardest on the homeless. Medical care was unavailable to the homeless.

Every day on the streets was a battle. Biting, hair-pulling and scratching were common modes of fighting. My favorite weapon was a rock, which is more compact than a stick. I always had a rock handy, since our gang had frequent run-ins with other gangs. The members of our gang were younger than some of the other gangs and I had a more difficult time because I looked very Caucasian. One day another group of street kids surrounded me. They hit me and knocked me to the ground. As they held me down, one put a flammable liquid on my arm and another boy lit it. They moved back to watch me burn. I stood up and bent my arm, perhaps instinctively to put out the flames, for I was in excruciating pain. When I opened my arm the fire had spread to the other side of my arm. Adult rescuers came and my attackers ran. An adult took a cloth and wrapped it around my arm and smothered the flames. Others picked me up, comforted me, dressed the wound, and fed me. They asked me many questions I could not answer. I did not know how old I was, my date of birth, where I lived, where any living relatives were. Later I was on the streets again, my arm wrapped. Forty-three years later I am reminded of how far I have come when I remove my shirt and see the third-degree burn scars of an incident that occurred when I was homeless and only five.

Not long afterward a Methodist missionary found me on the street. She was a young woman with long hair tied in a ponytail. Unlike my black hair, hers was light brown. I assume that I attracted her interest because I was obviously of mixed blood. She kneeled down, looked into my face and asked me the usual questions I could not answer: "Who are you…where are your parents, etc." She took my hand and we walked to an orphanage, called Choong Hyon Baby Home, located near a military installation. The buildings had been donated by the army for use as an orphanage. At the orphanage I was brought by the missionary to the headmistress. After asking me more questions, the headmistress opened a closet door. On the floor of the closet there was an immense pile of socks. I ran and jumped into the pile…I had found the "mother lode!" Both women laughed and told me I could take one pair of socks for my bare feet, just one pair. I was very grateful. It had been a long time since I had socks on my feet.

Orphanage Life

Life in the orphanage was not all peaches and cream but it was a great improvement over the hardships of living wild on the streets. There was a roof over my head. We were fed once a day, though this meal was very sparse due to lack of funding. However, we could at least rely on being fed each day. It was not unusual to go days without food when I was foraging in alleys. There was supervision in the orphanage. Of course, as in any institution, there were good people and there were bad people. I had my fair share of both.

The very first night I was in the orphanage I could not sleep. Many children were terrified. When the lights went out they screamed and cried. To get everyone to stop crying, older kids and adult staff walked up and down the rows of smaller kids, walking on the children's legs until everyone was quiet. A little boy lying next to me had a grin on his face. He lifted his covers to show me that by tucking your legs up tightly under your body until your knees touched your chest, one could avoid getting his legs walked upon. Then, if we were quiet and not crying, the older boys and staff would not hurt us. They would walk past. I learned many new ways to survive my new situation.

The next morning before anyone else awoke, I dressed and tried to get out the front door. It was locked! I was trapped! A counselor awoke, came up to me and asked me what I was doing. I told her I was "going fishing." I was certain that this was not the place for me and I wanted out! She laughed and told me I wasn't going anywhere.

At night someone often took my covers. It was very cold and I'd awaken in the morning shivering. A friend showed me how to tuck all the edges of my blankets up underneath myself so my body weight anchored the blankets and no one could steal them. It made us look like little mummies, but we would not shiver from the cold as a result of having our blankets stolen.

It was difficult living in the orphanage for several reasons. There was not enough money to take care of so many children; not enough clothing, shoes, or enough supervision. It was also very difficult for me to change from being wild and free on the streets, despite its dangers and tribulations, to a semi-controlled, poorly funded lifestyle in the orphanage. Also, the Korean workers in the orphanage shared the Korean people's disdain for biracial children.

However, there were some pleasant aspects to orphanage life besides a daily meal. For instance we were taught songs. We were organized to stand in long lines, sometimes two-by-two, sometimes single file. We'd walk to a nearby building singing songs while on our way to kindergarten. There were wooden trucks and blocks to play with and things to do. It was fun and we learned. In the playground there was a little merry-go-round.

I did not have to fight for my life against a group of starving street children, but I still had to fight one-on-one against individuals who were prejudiced because I was not 100% Korean.

Mealtime was often a test of strength. A typical meal started with the appearance of a cook bearing a large pan of what looked like uncooked bread dough. She dispensed it in pieces pulled from the pan to the children pushing around her. If you were small or weak the portion you got after the other children had grabbed their dough was sometimes pitifully small, not bigger than your thumb…and that was your daily meal. Of course this was happening at a time when Korea was desperately poor and trying to rebuild after the war. I have talked to Korean/Americans who lived in Korean orphanages during the 1960s and they have told me of getting three meals per day.

Sometimes we were taken into the field to help pick crops. The first time I was involved in picking I made the mistake of eating the string-bean-like vegetables I was supposed to pick. I got a beating in the field and, along with several other malefactors, subjected to a prolonged beating and other indignities that night at the orphanage.

Our toilet was downstairs in a basement where there were metal paint cans which served as toilets for the children. We sometimes hid in the basement though it was a very spooky place. At night when it was dark, kids who had misbehaved were confined there as a punishment. There were often cries of frightened children coming from the basement at night. We called it a dungeon. I had to spend a few nights there too.

Outside, next to the main sleeping quarters was a pond dammed

Earliest photo at the orphanage

by a concrete wall. We played near the spillway which was very slippery and difficult to cross. We'd roll up our pants and carefully creep along the ledge. One day a little girl fell into the pond and an older woman dove in to save her. It was not until forty years later that I found out who the girl was.

One day it was bath day. There was a metal tub filled with water that could fit up to eight children at one time. I was placed at the end of the line with the other biracial children. By the time it was my turn, the water was absolutely filthy. Some of the small children who had preceded me in the bath had soiled the water and I was horrified and did not want to be placed in the filth. I fought the bath attendant who attempted to force me into the water.

A big man picked me up by my ankles, carried me into another room which was surrounded by glass doors and windows, and slammed my head into the floor the way you would an animal you wanted to kill by breaking its neck. I was knocked out upon impact. I don't know how long I lay there unattended. When I finally came to, my face was stuck to the floor in a dried pool of my own blood. All the other kids had their faces pressed up against the glass, watching me from outside the room. The door opened and someone threw a towel at my head before slamming the door shut. This was not an act of kindness. I had to clean up the mess I had made on the floor. Later I was so body-sore that I am sure I had been thoroughly kicked while I was unconscious.

At such times I wanted to be free to roam the streets, to find my buddies who taught me how to survive, my friends who fought the old man until he let me go, my little buddies who grabbed me and ran me to safety. I missed them very much and may God watch over them and save a special place for them in heaven.

I was treated for TB while at the orphanage. Medical attention like that I would not have received had I been left on the streets. I had a mild case of measles and was cared for while sick, another plus for being in an orphanage. There were people with big hearts and there were people with no hearts. I guess it's like that all over the world. I hope children in the orphanages today are treated much better. The war was over forty-five years ago. Surely orphanages are better funded and equipped and the orphans are better cared for in Korea today.

Adoption

In 1956 the United States Congress passed an act which allowed Americans to adopt a stated number of Korean/American orphans from Korea. The first group of adoptees was airlifted to the safety of the U.S. and then the act expired. June and Richard Clement, two American citizens with very big hearts, heard about the plight of the war orphans left behind in Korea and decided that they too would adopt a Korean/American child. They had to wait until another Congressional act was passed, and when it was, they began the lengthy process of adoption which required family photographs, a family history and personal financial disclosure. My role during this process was that of "First Generation Korean/American Adoptee-In-Waiting."

When the people at the Choong Hyon Baby Home learned that I was the choice the Clement family was focusing on, my treatment changed drastically overnight. I became Adoptee Case #500. No more abuse. I was given close medical attention. They shaved my head to attend to the infection from the wound I had received from having my head slammed into the floor. In a report to the Clements they said that I had a ringworm which had to be surgically removed, requiring my head to be shaved. There were no other shaved heads in the orphanage. I was fed more, even got pudgy! I got to sit on someone's lap and try my first sip of coffee. People played with me and almost treated me as an equal!

In preparation for the adoption, an American military photographer was invited to the orphanage from a nearby army base to take my photograph. To induce me to smile, one of the orphanage staff positioned himself behind the photographer and did silly things like rolling on the floor. They took care to pose me in the best possible position and made sure my burn scars were not visible.

After the Clements made their final decision and picked ME!!!!!, there was a delay because my new mother, June, was pregnant with my future little sister, Leslie. After a successful delivery the adoption process was on!

It is interesting to note that the Clements religious affiliation is Methodist and that Tommy was found by a Methodist missionary nurse.

Although we do not yet know what will be the documentary requirements in intercountry adoption cases, we understand that the Clements would need to submit a copy of their marriage certificate; a copy of the birth certificate of one of them; an employment statement from Mr. Clement's employers, which should include information about his position, its permanence, and salary; a bank statement. We will be writing to confirm such documentation but thought the Clements might wish to begin assembling it if they are interested in Tommy and if you can approve his placement with them. We are enclosing two copies of:

                    STATEMENT OF ADOPTION
                    AFFIDAVIT OF SUPPORT

and two copies of:

These blanks need to be filled in and notarized in duplicate by the Clements and returned to us as they will be needed to obtain Tommy's passport in Korea. We would like to have these returned as soon as possible.

A portion of the pre-adoption documentation from the orphanage.

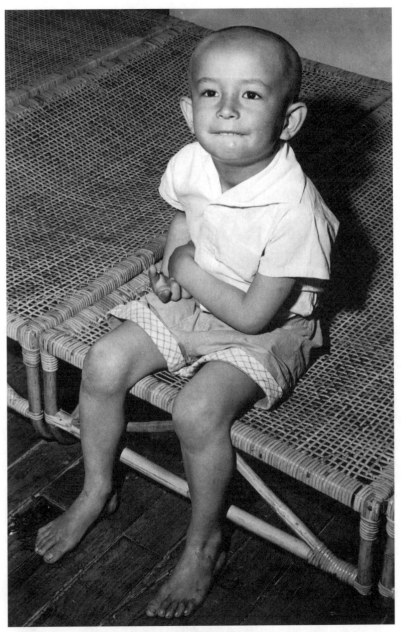

Photo with burn hidden

The very last day, when my escort arrived at the orphanage, I was dressed in new, donated clothes for my long journey to America. Someone took me aside and kneeling face-to-face with me, warned, "Don't you ever tell anyone about anything that happened here or we will come over there and bring you back."

I went with my escort to the airport for the journey. Another little waif, being adopted by an American family named Canada, was also to make the journey. In the plane I could not sit still; I ran up and down the aisles. Everyone was full of smiles and no one tried to hurt me.

SPORTS FINAL
★★

New York Mirror

SUNDAY, MAY 25, 1958

Tigers Top Yanks, 3-2

STORY ON PAGE 70

Giants, Dodgers Lose

STORIES ON PAGE 70

BASEBALL RESULTS

OUR TEAM		R H E
YANKEES.......	1 0 0 0 0 1 0 0 0—	2 7 1
Detroit	0 1 1 0 0 0 1 0 x—	3 8 0

MAGLIE, Ditmar (8) and Berra; LARY and Wilson.

AMERICAN LEAGUE		R H E
Baltimore	0 2 0 0 0 0 1 0 0—	3 9 2
Chicago	2 0 0 0 0 1 0 1 x—	4 8 0

O'DELL and Triandos; Keegan, FISCHER (6) and Lollar.

Washington	0 0 0 0 0 0 0 6 0—	6 8 2
Cleveland	0 0 2 1 0 0 0 0 0—	3 11 0

STOBBS, Byerly (8) and Korcheck; MOSSI, Garcia (8), Ferrarese (8) and Brown, Porter (8).

Boston.........	0 0 1 2 0 0 0 1 1—	5 8 1
Kansas City....	0 2 1 0 0 1 0 0 0—	4 10 1

Sullivan, WALL (8), Kiely (9) and White; Kellner, GORMAN (4) and Chiti.

NATIONAL LEAGUE		R H E
San Francisco ...	0 1 2 0 0 0 0 0 0—	3 8 1
Milwaukee	1 1 0 0 0 0 0 4 x—	6 10 0

McCormick, WORTHINGTON (6), Grissom (8) and Schmidt; Conley, McMAHON (8) and Crandall.

I came down the steps of the Northwest Orient Airlines plane at Idlewild Airport in New York City where my new father, Richard Clement, and Mrs. Canada were waiting. News photographers and photojournalists were ready. From the obscurity of the streets of Korea to the front page of the *New York Mirror*. Our pictures and stories went out across America.

My father gave me a tin friction-toy jeep and crayons. I liked the jeep best. At the time I was convinced that it was a *baby jeep* and it would grow into a full-size jeep. After many photos and interviews, my father and I continued on our trip by air to my new home in North Carolina. In Charlotte, North Carolina, we retrieved my father's car and departed on the last leg of the journey to my new home in Newton, North Carolina. As we drove I sat in the front with my father playing with the friction jeep on the dashboard. I guess I was getting a little wild with the new toy while my father was trying

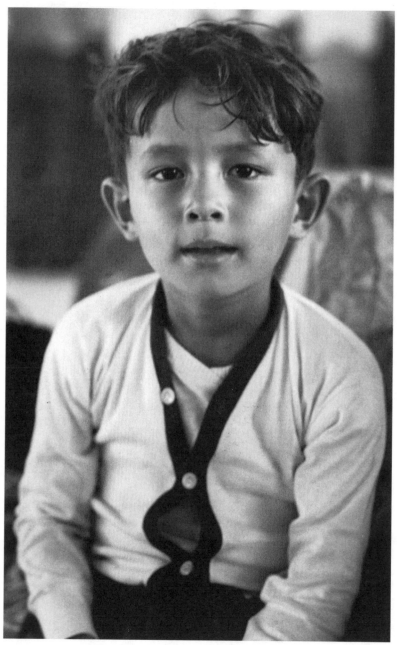

First day in America

to drive. He put up his hand to stop the jeep from falling onto the floor and he kept saying, "Easy...easy...easy...!!"

So I repeated what he was saying, "Easy...easy...easy...!!"

Later on in life he said, "The first English word you ever learned was 'easy' and I still don't think you know what it means!!!" Sorry Dad, *easy* is one of those relative words. I'm still trying to comprehend its meaning.

After what seemed like an endless journey, we arrived at our new home in Newton. One thing I immediately noted as being different from Korea was that no one removed their shoes when they entered the house.

There, I met my new mother, June. She was beautiful, and so warm and loving. This book is for you, Mom! I cannot thank my adoptive mother and father enough. You understand?

I was brought by my mother into the living room and placed in the middle of a huge soft couch. It was by far the largest thing to sit on that I had ever seen in my life! This thing was HUGE!!! My new younger brother, Richard, and my new older sister, Carolyn, were brought into the room to be introduced. They sat across from me and began to whisper to each other and giggle. It seemed that everyone was talking in a strange language. It sounded like Chinese. I did not comprehend that there was a language change between countries so I thought I had grown very stupid overnight. I could no longer understand anyone and no one could understand me. The Korean language was now obsolete. I wanted to go home.

EVERYTHING and I mean EVERYTHING was different. Lights were controlled by wall switches. I'd stand up on a chair and flip them on and off screaming "FIRE!" in Korean. When my mother came home with groceries it was "CHRISTMAS!!!" Why, these new people had Christmas every day! What a great place. My new home really wasn't that big by U.S. standards. It was a 1500-square-foot ranch-style house with three bedrooms. But Richard and I had a bedroom all to ourselves. Such luxury! When I awoke at night there were no strangers sleeping on the floor next to me. The house even had an attic where I could retreat when I needed quiet. And we had a basement with a high ceiling which we could bicycle in on rainy days. Talk about rich!

June Clement

At our very first family meal together I was seated in a chair with my chin almost level with my plate. There were no chopsticks. How the heck was I supposed to eat? Spoons were a lot easier and less dangerous than a pointed fork; forks were "ouchy." The food that was piled up on my plate was absolutely amazing. I thought it was the serving plate and I was supposed to take a little of it. Eventually I got with the program and ate my food. After I had eaten more than I had ever eaten in one sitting, I got confused. My mother was trying to ask me something I could not comprehend. Different people at the table kept asking and trying to communicate a very bizarre concept that I just could not comprehend...*seconds*! They were trying to ask me if I wanted seconds. What in the world were *seconds*??? Why would anyone want to eat right after they just ate? Now I know what seconds are, even thirds, snacks, hors d'oeuvres, and desserts. What a strange country. I thought, "I just might like it here."

My mother offered me some chocolate pudding for dessert. I absolutely refused. Yuck! We all know what chocolate pudding looks like. She held it close to my nose to smell. I held my breath and shook my head.

My parents thought I was very insecure because I would not wander beyond our property line. Actually, I was terrified that I would get separated from my new family and never see them again. These things happen, you know.

The first time I heard my father's voice on the phone I jumped back from the phone. Wow! My new dad had somehow gotten stuck in this little thing. I had a sinking feeling I would never see him again. Was I ever happy when he came home safe that night!

Everything was so new and different. Television. My mother turned on the television and walked into the kitchen. I couldn't believe my eyes and ears. A large box with lights and knobs and sound. I had to inspect this thing. After looking at it carefully, I stepped back two feet to observe the program on the screen. On the television screen was a "Cowboy and Indians" show. First there were angry words; it looked like a confrontation. I liked the Indians because they had colorful painted faces and beautiful feathers in their hair. They were riding horses which were also new to me. Then the

Carolyn, Leslie, Richard & Tommy

unspeakable happened. One Indian, whom I particularly liked, was riding toward the cowboys and a cowboy shot my Indian friend right off his horse...right in front of my face. I burst into tears, ran into the kitchen, grabbed my mother's skirt and pulled her into the living room. I was blubbering. She couldn't understand at first why I was so upset, and then she knew. For me this wasn't entertainment. In my life, shooting people was for real. The dead didn't rise again. She turned off the television, held and caressed me and managed to divert my attention to other more happy pursuits, like cookies. I must not have been traumatized by this unique experiment (transporting a child from a war-torn culture, sans television, to an advanced industrialized nation) because within weeks I was playing "Cowboys and Indians" with my peers in the field behind our home and insisting on getting my share of being cowboy. I also soon learned to sit unafraid in front of our television, eating a banana or apple, while cartoon characters and real people assaulted each other. The playful punishment inflicted by the "Three Stooges" on each other became understandable to me. I was now able to distinguish between the real and the imaginary.

Speaking of bananas and apples, my mother had no trouble tracking the banana peels which I deposited around the house, until she taught me where the trash receptacle was. But she could not track down my apple cores. That is, until she found several apple *stems*. I ate my apples street-style, starting at the end of the apple opposite the stem, and I kept going until I reached the stem. Nothing was wasted! If I had been exposed to bananas in Korea, I might have eaten the banana peels too.

After I had been with my new family for a couple of months my mother decided to invite some Korean students from a nearby college to find out what had happened to me in Korea. Perhaps inviting Korean-speaking students to meet me would be an excellent way to find out... a Korean talking to a Korean. Some students duly arrived and one knelt in front of me, face to face, and asked, "Tommy, what happened in Korea?"

She was the first Korean I had seen since I had left Korea. *My hair stood up on the back of my neck.* "My God," I thought, "they have come over here and are testing me to see if I tell, and if I do they will take me back with them to Korea!" I answered, "Nossing...jess nossing." I did not want to answer any questions, nor even to talk to them. I wanted to hide behind my mother's dress. I did not want to go back to the orphanage. I did not want to go back to the war.

As a result of this incident my mother wrote an entry in my childhood scrapbook which stated that I must have had an "uneventful" life in Korea. The fact is, many times children respond to a parental question only after they have analyzed what the answer should be, not what the truth is.

My first English word was, "Easy...easy...easy!" Some others were, "Holy Smoke" and "Hands OFF!" I guess I was a little hyper as a child. I must have seemed like a strange kid.

Running water from faucets was fantastic. I washed my hands over and over again. Indoor plumbing, what an invention. Of course the tub was very scary, but the sink was manageable. My mother had to coax me away from the sink with cookies.

Adjusting to the days in my new home was much easier than the nights. During the day it was light and my mind could assimilate my new surroundings. I'd block out bad thoughts and not think about things that bothered me. I could concentrate on learning and playing. The nights were totally different. Everyone else went to sleep; they went away. When the lights went out I could not block out bad thoughts. It didn't matter that my new brother was asleep in the same room. Recurring nightmares haunted me. I would awaken screaming and sweating. When my brother Richard was forty-four years old he told me how I used to wake him at night howling.

The bed! I could not balance myself on the bed. I would crash to the floor, sometimes hitting my head. My new parents, seeing my problem, placed a mattress on the floor for me to sleep. Then I kept falling off the mattress and they would still find me in the morning on the floor. The solution was a couch that my parents turned backwards against the wall so I *couldn't* fall off.

When I fell asleep, there they were: flashing skies from the bombing, air raid sirens, ear-deafening booms, people screaming and running, large wheels of army trucks in the streets, wounded people being helped along. The German Shepherd army dogs were terrifying. And one poor man's face I kept seeing over and over again drenched in blood. He could not move; his head tilted to one side. The image of two rifles leaning up against a wall flickered as the bombing illuminated them. I hated going to sleep. I would wake up screaming, jump out of bed, run down the darkened hallway, burst into my parents' room and jump into their bed. It was safer there; I knew they would protect me. They were good people with big hearts. Sometimes they would let me stay; sometimes they brought me back to my couch-bed. I would lie, my eyes open, my ears ringing, and watch the shadows. The night-light they had placed in the bedroom was comforting. As my eyes adjusted to the dim light I could convince myself I was no longer in the war.

Sometimes when everyone was asleep and I was afraid, I would go into the living room, turn on the TV and watch the test pattern until the TV station woke up and started their shows. There was "Captain Kangaroo" with the always hilarious *Banana Man* who never ran out of bananas. He kept pulling them out of his coat pockets. I still like the *Banana Man*. Once there was an Asian news reporter on the TV. I stopped playing and paid close attention. I was okay though…as no one had come out of that little box yet. As I grew up, the nightmares became less frequent. However, I'm 47, and after 40 years I still have recurrences. Most people have never been in a war. I hope they never are. I wouldn't recommend it for anyone.

After all these years I cannot think about some things without being overcome with grief. I cannot read some of my international e-mail from friends overseas. It would frighten me to do a live interview. If I attempted to do it I would risk being publicly overcome by grief.

School Daze

Three months after I arrived in the U.S. my father was transferred by his employer, The General Electric Company, from North Carolina to Pittsfield, Massachusetts. Our new home was in a neighborhood near a dairy farm in the Berkshire hills. The dairy farm actually bordered our rear yard. Sometimes the cows got through the fence and wandered into our yard. At such times, my mother would sound the alarm, "Cows in the yard" and we all ran to help. Even Leslie, who was quite small at the time, grabbed a broom and shooed the cows back across the brook that ran through our backyard onto the farm property.

I settled into my new home with no apparent problem. Only many years later my mother told me that a man who lived several doors away had circulated a petition protesting the introduction of an Amerasian child into the neighborhood. Luckily, he got little support.

After we got settled in our new home, I entered the first grade at Williams Elementary School without knowing how to speak more than a few words of English. A neighbor, Mrs. van den Honert, saw my plight and volunteered to tutor me in the phonics method of reading. She did this faithfully for several years and I will always remember her kindness.

At school I had a hard time adjusting. When I got frustrated I hid under my desk. My first grade teacher told my parents on Parents Day, "Little Tommy spends more time under his desk than at his desk." Perhaps I was practicing for air raids. I felt a little more secure with a desk over my head, that's all. Needless to say I received very poor grades. My first grade report card contained a steady parade of "U"s (U for unsatisfactory) with only an occasional "I" (improvement needed). Actually, I blazed a new trail in American education by getting a "U minus" in one instance.

My second grade performance was not much better. Once when we had a math test, I copied the paper of a good friend who sat next to me. After the teacher graded the papers she handed them back and

Leslie shooing cows

said, "Here's a paper for Christopher van den Honert. Very good, Christopher! And here's another paper for Christopher van den Honert. Very good, Christopher! And...where is your paper, Tommy?" She knew. I didn't realize what had happened until later. I had copied Christopher's whole paper including his name.

I learned some concepts very quickly though. I learned that it was good to get good grades and it was bad to get bad grades. I learned that when taking a test you were supposed to put your name at the top of the paper, not your friend's name from whose paper you were copying. Once, when I received a very bad grade on a math test, I asked to go to the boys' room and flushed my bad paper down the toilet. I couldn't bring it home! When I got back in my seat, the teacher asked me, "Where is your paper, Tommy?" I answered, "I don't know." She motioned to me with her index finger to follow her. We walked to the boys' room. There, floating in the toilet because it would not go down, was my very bad test with my name in large letters, "Tommy Clement." I was then escorted down to the principal's office where kindly Miss Coffey gave me a lecture about the school's plumbing system and how expensive it is to fix if broken with my bad papers. Plumbing is a wonderful thing. When it breaks it's a terrible thing.

Language was the most difficult barrier to my integration into my new wonderful world. I had trouble expressing my feelings and didn't know that language was the problem. I had a feeling that it wasn't language, but my limited intelligence. I thought I was stupid.

Birthdays were another strange concept. My mother asked, "What age are you going to be this year?" Because she had asked I thought I got to choose my age. I answered, "I be ten, okay, so I can be same as Carolyn." She burst into laughter.

During my first birthday party when kids brought me presents, I pushed all the presents into a corner to make sure they wouldn't be taken home by the guests. A sense of sharing is not something inherent; it was something I had to learn.

I loved dinner time because everyone in the family sat down together. Our family took turns going around in a circle, each one saying a letter of the alphabet so that I would learn my A B C's. There is a song to help little children learn their A B C's. When it got to be my turn, I said, "LMNO" as one letter because in the song, "LMNO" sounded like one letter. The whole family would rock with laughter.

I was reminded of this later on in years when I was older and Johnny Carson had a little boy on his show. The boy had drawn a beautifully detailed picture of Jesus in the Manger. There was a little round depiction of a person in the lower right corner. Johnny asked, "And who is this?" pointing to the little figure. The little boy answered, "Why, that's RoundJohnVirgin."

My father was sometimes like Johnny Carson. He would smile and tell us jokes at dinner. Of course he edited them for us. One joke was about a man who left the factory where he worked every day with a wheelbarrow heaped with straw. And every day the guard at the factory gate stopped him and meticulously went through the straw looking for something hidden. But the guard never found anything and let the man go by. After weeks and weeks of this, the guard

Family portrait in Pittsfield, Mass.

Tommy and Richard catching fish

became frustrated that he could never find anything and finally asked, "I know you're taking something...what is it? I promise I won't tell anyone if you only tell me!" The man leaned over to him and said, "I'm taking wheelbarrows." At dinner we were always asked how our day went. Dinner was a wonderful time for our family to bond and learn about each other. Richard usually sat next to our dad and I usually sat next to our mom. My sisters sat across from us.

Although I wasn't always well-behaved at dinner, I do remember thinking that my brother and sisters sometimes pushed their luck by being unruly. I thought to myself, "This life is good. I am not going to risk being disinvited. I am going to keep a low profile."

There were no other Korean children in Pittsfield that I was aware of, let alone another Korean/American adoptee. Though I felt loved by my parents and siblings, I felt most secure spending time alone in fields behind our house. Streams ran through the fields and right across the back of our building lot. My happiest hours were spent catching rainbow and speckled trout with my hands or a fishing rod, then dressing and freezing them so that our family could have a trout dinner. My mother showed me how to roll the fish in flour, heat up cooking oil and cook the fish. They were delicious.

My favorite day was the day fishing season opened. I would wake up before dawn and sit on the back step with my fishing rod and worms. As soon as it was light I was fishing. There were others fishing besides myself, including adults with $500 rods and $500 reels plus waders, nets, etc. I knew the favorite hiding spots for the fish and knew that fish were territorial, each fish having a little domain. With my $10 rod and reel, and sometimes just using a hand line, I would begin pulling fish out immediately. The other fishermen would say, "That little SOB, that pipsqueak, how does he do that?" I didn't mind; they were on my territory! In fact, I knew that where they were fishing there were no fish!

Much of my childhood was spent playing by myself in the woods nearby our house, making weapons and hiding them throughout the hills. I made knives from "bandits" lying around house construction sites and little huts out of sticks and sod. I was a loner, slow in learning to play with others. I felt better alone with nature because my perceived ignorance was not a factor in the hills and woods. No one was there to pass judgment; there was no "program." I was free to observe nature, the bugs, the animals, the trees. I was free and capable.

At times, I had the feeling I was an alien again, a *tuki* (alien devil). Not only because the adoption papers said so, but because deep down inside I felt I was. I always kept an eye out for the crash site of my flying saucer. Sometimes I'd stand on a mountain ledge at attention, looking straight ahead. I'd turn my body around in a complete circle as though relaying my whereabouts back to my mother planet. I did this well into my late teens. Weird.

At a fairly early age I became a tinkerer. If anything had parts, gears or hinges I loved to take it apart and understand how it worked. My parents encouraged this interest by spreading newspaper out on the dining room table and giving Richard and me large old clocks to disassemble with screwdrivers. Unlike many parents who would

Backyard bounty

have thrown away an old broken clock, they saved them in a box in the bottom of the front closet so that we could use them as learning projects. They were very supportive parents.

However, my reading rate was very poor; every word was pronounced in my mind as I read. My little sister Leslie had surpassed me in reading speed. She was reading Harlequin novels while I was still laboring through "Puff the Magic Dragon." Sometimes I couldn't even understand what people were saying so I was often quiet. I was held back in fifth grade because I was doing so poorly academically. The school felt I was not ready to progress to the next grade.

One Monday morning in sixth grade I knew I was in trouble when I got to school. The teacher walked me over to my desk. There was a terrible fishy smell emanating from my desk. He opened it up. I had made the ends in a little pencil tray watertight by squeezing Silly Putty into the cracks. Then I had filled the tray from the water fountain. During recess I gathered polliwogs and aquatic swamp

Richard, Cari, June

plants and pebbles from a stream near the school and made a little indoor, in-desk aquarium. As the teacher lectured I would lift my desk top from time to time and enjoy my little friends swimming around. However, over the weekend the water leaked out and the little critters dried up and smelled to high heaven. I never did that again. But just in case my teacher went into my desk again, I took an empty sewing thread spool with two sticks placed at opposite ends of the spool connected together by a rubber band through the hole in the spool, wound the two sticks like a propeller and carefully placed the spool in the tray before closing the lid. Anyone but me who opened the desk would have been very surprised!

I must have impressed someone in school because before I graduated from sixth grade, my teacher took me aside and said, "Tommy, I think you are an exceptionally smart person." I thought he was exceptionally ignorant because I knew how dumb I was.

Our family found themselves in some political difficulty before I graduated from elementary school. When I was twelve, my parents received a notification that I was being drafted into the South Korean Army! At that time boys were automatically drafted. In my case a mistake must have been made because I was very young. What my new parents had overlooked was that although I was adopted, I was still a Korean citizen. After much *to-do* they obtained my American citizenship. I received a letter from one of the Kennedys congratulating me. It was signed with an original signature. We sent the letter to the Korean Army to prove to them that I was now an untouchable—I was an American.

The Great Escape

One of my favorite movies as a child was *The Great Escape* starring Steve McQueen. In this movie U.S. captive soldiers hid things in a hollowed-out book which was then placed back on a shelf in plain view. I was about 12 years old at the time. Without permission, which would have defeated the point, I went to my parents' bookshelves that straddled both sides of the fireplace and chose a very wide book to hollow out. The book was *Etiquette* by Emily Post. It was one of my mother's books from Smith College. With book in hand I found a razor blade of my dad's, went up to the bedroom and started cutting the center of the pages out, leaving a one-inch border around the edges of each page. This took a long time; there were many pages. Eventually the project was completed and I placed some of my favorite stones, a jackknife and coins into its secret compartment before placing the book in my headboard bookshelf.

You must remember that throughout my childhood I was relatively quiet. My parents did not know what was going on in my little brain. After a few months had lapsed I was called one evening to the living room. My father was reading a newspaper in his favorite lounge chair and my mother was sitting on the couch. To my dismay she had my secret book in her lap. She asked, "Why did you do this to my book?"

I looked at her and answered, "Because I thought it was ingenious."

With a very straight face she handed the book to me! I took it and thanked her, turned around and left. Behind me I could hear both my mother and father laughing. They had never heard me use such a large word, let alone in such an appropriate manner. They could have punished me for ruining her college textbook. Instead, they were tickled pink that I had done this alteration and used such an excellent English word when confronted.

My family called me a pack rat. A pack rat brings home anything that isn't tied down. My multiple-pocketed shorts were always filled with a variety of small trinkets found by the side of the road or from the creeks and woods I roamed. My parents and siblings thought it was amusing. One day I said to my father, who had asked me questions about Korea, "We had nossing...jess' nossing." So, I was simply amazed that the prized junk that I had gathered from around my new home was absolutely FREE! It was lying around the ground for the taking. At forty-seven years old I am still this way. So beware! If it's not glued down, watch out. To this day my barn, garage and my rooms are cluttered with reminders of our throw-away society. What a land of plenty. If you are born and raised here it is taken for granted. If you are not born here you will be forever amazed at the STUFF!

America is so rich. Even a simple thing like Pennies for UNICEF (United Nations Children's Emergency Fund) can generate great sums of money for charity. My mother was the City of Pitts-field's, and later Berkshire County's, Pennies for UNICEF coordinator for many years. The annual penny drive in Berkshire County raised over $4,000 once my mother got things organized. That is 400,000 pennies, and my family did the sorting and wrapping of all that. We opened all the little UNICEF donation cartons and dumped the contents into an incredible pile on our living room carpet. Then my brother, Richard, and I tried to look at every penny collected, searching for mint-years that we needed for our coin collections. Our hands were black by the time we got through. I still have my treasured penny coin collection from that period. It gives me a little chill to view those coins and remember my family sorting and pack-aging those pennies together on our living room floor on Mountain Drive.

In the summers we visited my maternal grandmother in her cot-tage in the Adirondack Mountains. Grandma's two sisters lived in an old house nearby. Thus, by being adopted by the Clements, I ac-quired more than parents and siblings. I also got a grandmother and Aunt Edie and Aunt Nettie...and uncles and cousins. This was on my mother's side of our family. I also acquired a grandmother, grand-father, uncles, aunts and cousins on my father's side, but they were further away and I saw them less often. Learning everyone's name and keeping track of who was brother or sister to whom was very difficult for me.

Grandma's cottage in the Adirondacks gave me more opportu-

Tea with Aunt Edie (middle) and relatives

nity to roam, often stopping for tea with Aunt Edie and Aunt Nettie. We even installed a battery-operated telephone line between our two houses so we children could make tea dates with our aunts. Everybody in our extended family made me welcome. Americans have good hearts and adoptees are accepted as a normal, desirable means of enriching family life. The presumption is that the adoptee is a resource to be cultivated and enjoyed.

While going to elementary school I did many typical American things after school hours. I joined the Boy Scouts of America but could never catch on to that program either. I think I may have been the only one to remain a Tenderfoot for two years. I never had the motivation to progress beyond a Tenderfoot because you had to read stuff for that. Richard and I subscribed to a Boy Scout magazine called *Boys' Life*. My little sister Leslie read these magazines even more than I did because she liked the heroic true-life stories which were featured in each month's edition.

When two other Tenderfeet and I spent a weekend camping we decided to pretend that we were undergoing survival training. I showed the other two how to catch fish with their hands and by throwing spears and rocks. We chanced upon a large patch of blackberries, dug wild onions, found apple and pear trees. We ate crayfish, frog legs, cattail stalks, pine tree seeds and anything else we could get our hands on. We ate and ate. Survival amidst the abundance of the Berkshire Hills was no problem for me. All you needed was the good sense to know when to stop eating.

My brother and I each had a paper route. We usually accompanied each other because our routes were adjacent to each other. In the fall we would return home via a nearby cornfield where early frost sometimes kept the corn in a surprisingly fresh state, long after the field had been harvested. We left home with our paper bags full of papers and returned with them full of corn. This was perfectly natural for me, living off the land.

Behind our house was a dairy farm with fields, forests, and many brooks filled with trout. We spent a lot of time playing in the fields. Kippy, John and I went into a dry field one spring. My friends did not believe I could start a fire by focusing a magnifying glass on a dry leaf, but it only took a few seconds and there it was, a little fire. The wind rose and the little fire turned into raging, completely out of control fire. You know the saying, "like wild fire?" Well this was one hell of a wild fire. Kippy had the sense to run home and notify his parents who called other neighbors and the fire department. We were all out there fighting the blaze. My sister Leslie was also there trying to help us. She exclaimed, "Gee! This is just like *Boys' Life*! Real Boy Scouts putting out a real fire!"

John turned to her and said, "Yea, a real Boy Scout STARTED it!"

By the time the fire was out the entire field was burned. Everyone went home except me. I had to stay behind and sit in the burned field as punishment. I thought about how I had made many fires with a magnifying glass, but never with this result. What was different about this? The wind! The wind had fanned a small fire into a huge one.

There was a rustling noise coming across the burned field. It was the farmer! I thought I was going to have to fight him. I stood up and got ready. He stood next to me gazing across the black field. After some moments he said, "You know, it's against the law for me to burn my field. People don't understand that I can't mow down the dead stuff because the terrain is too bumpy for that. You know, burning is the best way to clear all the years of dead vegetation so that the new can grow." He looked across to another, unburned field and said thoughtfully, "If you ever get a hankerin' to do it again, that one over there could sure use it." He strolled away.

That year the burned field was more beautiful than it had ever been. The grass grew thick and tall, and the wildflowers grew like never before. Of course, I never took him up on his offer.

In the middle of junior high school I came down with rheumatic fever. One morning I awakened and my knee was swollen. I could not bend it. My mother brought me to our family doctor, Dr. Sullivan, who asked, "Did you hit your knee or did you just wake up like this?"

I answered, "I just woke up like this." He immediately took me to Pittsfield General Hospital, did a sedimentary rate analysis on my blood and confirmed that I had rheumatic fever. I stayed in the hospital for what seemed like weeks. In the hospital I remember blacking out. After a long stay in bed the nurses had told me not to get out of bed without help. I got out of bed anyway and walked to the window because I wanted to see outside. Everything went into slow motion and I started falling backwards. Dust particles floating in the air were as clear as though under a microscope; sounds were muffled and my vision narrowed to tunnel vision and then—nothingness. I awoke back in bed. A nurse was standing there holding my hand.

After being released from the hospital I had to stay in my bedroom at home for months. My friends collected money for me so that I could buy my very first electric guitar. I had a private tutor so as not to fall behind in school. A very important math aptitude test was coming up. My friends took the test first and came to visit me and told me all the questions that they could remember from the test. I would not have done as well without their help.

When I was around 14 years old neighbor kids came running to my house. They knew that I was very good at catching wild animals and was an outdoor woodsman. They were yelling about a big rat in their garage.

I took a homemade cage with me and walked back with them to their house. There it was: a huge rat, a little larger than a house cat, running back and forth in their garage. I opened the cage and placed it along the back wall. Rats prefer dark places and stay close to corners or walls when possible. With stick in hand I chased the rat into the cage and locked the cage door so we could safely inspect our catch. The rat had large cuts all over its back and was covered with maggots wriggling about in the cuts. It looked like the rat was foaming at the mouth—a good sign that it was rabid. Since it was probably rabid, it had to be shot.

With my brother's single-shot air rifle in hand and the other kids following me, we walked into a nearby field, the same field I had burned down as a younger kid. We placed the cage fifteen feet from where the gun lay waiting. One of the kids stood next to the cage. I walked over to the rifle and made sure it was loaded. The little boy opened the cage door and ran.

I looked through the rifle's scope and took aim. The scope was so powerful that the rat appeared as big as an elephant! The problem was, it did not sit still. When the door opened it came running straight at me. When a rat runs, it is not like in cartoons, where its body stays stationary and only the little feet move, scurrying along. This rat hopped, not small hops, but big hops, and fast…and directly toward me! I kept trying to keep the rat's head in my crosshairs, but had to move the barrel up and down as it hopped, very quickly, straight at me. I could not get a shot off.

Eventually it ran right up to me so I had to hit it with the end of the rifle. It fell over onto its side. Without looking through the scope I placed the barrel next to it and shot it dead.

The other kids were very happy. One little girl said, "I thought it was going to bite you." It would have if I hadn't hit it with the end of the rifle. We buried it in the woods and made a little wooden cross for it.

Junior and Senior High School

Junior high school in New England was grades seven through nine. I was in the lower caliber classes for students with learning problems. There was a special reading room to help special students and it was always embarrassing to enter because other students knew about this room. In the reading classroom there were state-of-the-art machines to help speed up one's reading rate. A machine scrolled down a written page at any speed you dialed in, with a single sentence visible at any one time. Later this method was abandoned for a more peripheral approach.

One day when I was still in junior high school a friend told me that a group of young toughs were going to "kick my Korean ass." This was a group of hoods who were well-known at my school. I knew that they smoked. When I got home I went up into my bedroom to prepare. I took a hole-punch and punched the gunpowder out of a roll of caps normally used in cap guns. After placing the powder into an empty .22 shell, I used a wooden artist paintbrush handle to tamp it down. With all my strength I pressed down on the brush handle. It blew up in my face. The sound was impressive. I inspected my face in a mirror and saw a piece of the wooden handle sticking out of my forehead. Thankfully it had not penetrated deeply, but my forehead was bleeding and my face was speckled with soot from the explosion. Over the loud ringing in my ears I could hear my mother's voice from downstairs, "Tom, are you okay up there?"

Still looking at the wooden "antenna" sticking from my forehead, I yelled back, "I'm fine, Mom," and pulled the piece of wood from my head before proceeding to the bathroom to wash up.

I then punched more gunpowder from a new roll of caps, placed the powder on a piece of paper and rolled it all into a tight cylinder which I fastened with Scotch tape. I emptied a cigarette, placed the load inside, replaced the tobacco and packed it tightly. The loaded cigarette was then placed back into the full pack of cigarettes.

I was standing at the back of the school when my tormentors approached me. First they dumped my books onto the ground. Then

43

one of them held my arms behind my back while the other three slapped me in the face and called me names. One, named Ricky, went through my pants pockets looking for money and found nothing. He went into my top shirt pocket and found the cigarettes which he took before punching me in the stomach. I fell to the ground and the boy who had held my arms kicked me in the back. They laughed and called me a "gook" before wandering off.

Two years later I learned from Ricky, with whom I had become friends in the meantime, that after they harassed me they went down the street to a local restaurant, had some soft drinks, spaghetti and then of course, cigarettes. It was Ricky who lucked out and got the cigarette with the load in it. While his friends were still eating, the cap powder exploded, spraying smoke and tobacco all over Ricky and startling everyone in the restaurant. The owner of the restaurant kicked them all out. They thought the whole thing was very funny and decided to leave me alone. Later we became friends as Ricky wanted me to show him how to make loaded cigarettes.

In junior high school I also had a run-in with a boy named Red. He was a good five inches taller than I and was robust. I, on the other hand, was slight, almost skinny. I was standing with three girls and a boy. Hanging around girls was a new thing with me. Red came up to us with a couple of his friends. He pressed his hands to the sides of his temple and pulled the skin taut which made his eyes look more like mine. He stuck his front teeth out and gurgled some sounds like he was trying to sound Asian. He called me a "Chink" and left laughing with his friends. That night I began to practice in front of the bathroom mirror. I locked the door and used my fingers to open my eyes as wide as I could until it hurt. I examined my eyes so closely that my nose touched the mirror. Yes, Red was right, my eyes did not look like his. I looked like I was smiling all the time. He, on the other hand, looked like he had seen a ghost. I needed to see more ghosts.

But I still did not understand why anyone would ridicule me for looking different. I still don't. When I encounter ridicule of this sort I remember that there is a land far away where I perhaps belong...among a family I might never see again.

In seventh grade I joined my first rock and roll group. The Beatles were fairly new and few kids in our city owned electric guitars.

A few of us who did have them in junior high school practiced in basements of homes where the parents were tolerant of loud music. We had more energy than talent but it sure was fun.

When I got older I met Jeff Johnson, an ambitious bass player who wanted more than anything in life to form a rock and roll band. He looked like a clone of the famous rock musician, Jimi Hendrix. The only difference between Jimi and Jeff was that Jimi had talent and Jeff played bass, not lead guitar. Jeff found out from a high school buddy of his that I played lead guitar and even more importantly, I owned my own equipment—a guitar and an amplifier. Jeff and I quickly became buddies. Jeff was so proud of his new "lead player" that he took me around to all of his friends and introduced me. He would say, "Brotha James, I want you to meet MY new lead player. Tom, meet brotha James." Minutes later Jeff would say, "Sista Janet, I want you to meet MY new lead player. Tom, this is sista Janet."

This went on for three weeks. I finally said, "Jeff, I've seen large families before. Mr. Sacco has twelve kids. The Jays up in North River have nine. Tell me, how in the world did your mother have so many kids?" He must have introduced me to over 50 brothas and sistas. How in the world was this possible?

At first he didn't understand my question. Then, with a gleam in his eye he looked at me and said, "Brotha TOM!" From that moment on I understood...we are all blood.

I began to hang out with Jeff and a singer, Jimmy, who was Turkish. We were probably the first minority ecumenical rock and roll band in the area. We were a bit crazy. Let me elaborate, we were VERY crazy. None of us were particularly interested in school at the time. As musicians we thought we were too cool! Boy, did we sound terrible! What we lacked in talent we over-compensated for in loudness and enthusiasm. This was the beginning of my rock and roll career. We played our music in one hall after another. Traveling took up quite a bit of time, which didn't help our school grades any. We even played on a local TV show which really boosted our recognition. We became a member of the music union. The rules were, if we missed a gig, we were fined for the amount we were to be paid plus we'd have to play there in the future for free. It was double jeopardy.

We did not want to miss a gig. It was a good policy to discourage no-shows.

Playing gigs was great. It was a real rush standing in front of a bunch of neopubescent girls who must have thought we were cute; it couldn't have been the quality of our music. The din was unbelievable. It was positively hormonal!

I had a misunderstanding with my parents as a result of my career as a musician. I had never explained the musician union rules to my parents. One weekend my band was scheduled to play and my parents had made plans to go to Cape Cod for a week on the beach. My parents insisted that I was going so we could be together as a family. I insisted adamantly that I was not, offering no explanation for my refusal. I had been my usual moody self during this period and had sassed my mother more times than my father could countenance. The upshot was that my father kicked me out of the house. He opened the screen door and announced, "Straighten out or leave!" I left and moved in with Jeff's family, who took me in with no questions asked. We played that weekend, got paid, and went on to other gigs.

A little later I returned home for some clothes and my father asked if I had enough money. I proudly answered "Yes" (we had been paid) and I departed.

Two weeks after that I asked my father if I could return home since I had run out of money by then. He said, "Tom, stick it out until school starts in the fall. I think that would be best for all of us." I did stick it out by moving in with some fellow musicians and nothing was said about the matter when I did return home.

The next summer, my brother, Richard, told me that he was contemplating moving out of our house for the summer. I told him, "Richard, you are crazy. Here at home, Mom cooks for you and does your laundry, Dad gives you an allowance and you get to use the car. If you move out you will be broke and find yourself living with kids who have even lower hygiene standards than you do." He stayed at home. Years later when I first heard the term "Tough Love" mentioned, I thought to myself, "Been there, done that!"

Our band was hired to play in New York City. Jeff drove because at the time I did not have a car. In the middle of Harlem Jeff decided that he had to have some Kentucky Fried Chicken, so we pulled into a KFC parking lot. Jeff was a huge guy of color. We sat in the parking lot for a long time arguing which of us would go and buy the food. He argued that it was his car and he was doing all the driving so I should go in.

As soon as I got out of the car, Jeff leaned over and locked my door. I didn't appreciate this one bit. What if, for some reason, I had to run back to the car to jump in? I walked over to the driver's side window. He lowered his window only an inch.

"Jeff, unlock the door," I said. He shook his head. "Unlock the Goddamned door or I'm not going in to buy the food."

"I'm not going to unlock the door until you get the food," he answered.

I realized that I was stuck. Apprehensively, I went into the store, stood in line with everyone looking at me and ordered the food without incident. But, back in the car, I realized that Jeff had been as afraid to get out of the car in Harlem as I was.

I even played in a band with Kenny Aronoff, who later became a drummer renowned throughout the U.S. That is my claim to fame: I played in the worst band that Kenny ever played with. One of the jobs booked with Kenny was in the Catskill Mountains at a Jewish camp. The fee was $450, which was a lot of money in those days. We threw together what musicians we could find. We had never practiced as a group; we just met at the camp and played loud.

At one in the morning we packed up our gear and left. Kenny left first with his drums loaded into his yellow convertible Mustang. That was the last time I saw him until 20 years later. I rode with Jimmy Hanna in his convertible Corvette followed by Jeff, our bass player, driving an old Chevy. Jeff had a lead foot.

When Jimmy and I rounded a sharp bend in the road that trailed down the mountain, Jim brought our car to an abrupt stop. He said, "Jeff isn't going to make it around that corner!" He began to back up. "I'd better park over here on this side of the road so he doesn't hit us," Jimmy said. He parked the car and sprinted up the hill to the sharp corner with me trailing him. Standing there in the dark on a lonely country road felt like something in the "Twilight Zone" TV series. Sure enough, Jeff came around the corner, went off of the road, knocked down seven traffic posts like dominoes, and then smashed into a large rock. On impact he lifted his right arm to his eyes and screamed. The car throttle stuck on full speed. The car's engine was extremely loud as Jeff jumped out of the car and ran over to us.

Jimmy yelled, "Everybody get away from the car. It's going to blow!" We started backing away. "Hey Tom, go up there and turn it off!" Jimmy called. I walked up to the car and got into the driver's seat. I couldn't find the ignition key. The sound of the racing engine plus the steam and smoke disoriented me but I finally located the key and shut the engine off. Silence. Luckily, Jeff wasn't badly hurt. His car was *totaled*.

When I reached the 9th grade I was introduced to the wonderful world of electronics. I wanted a better guitar amp. Most kids go out and buy a guitar amp. My father suggested that I buy a HeathKit. These were electrical kits, a guitar amplifier for instance, which were purchased by mail and delivered to your doorstep completely disassembled. Even the decals on the front panel had to be pasted on. A schematic of the assembly of electronic components and metal cabinetry was included. All you needed was a screwdriver, a soldering iron, solder and a lot of patience. I sat for hours assembling a shortwave radio, a stereo amplifier, a guitar amplifier and speaker cabinets for my dad and myself. It was an excellent education. It also cost less to buy things disassembled than assembled. Of course, sometimes when I finished a project and plugged it in, it would expire in a cloud of smoke and I'd have to send the whole thing back to the HeathKit company. They would then troubleshoot the thing and fix it for $50 no matter how badly it was damaged.

Reading electronics manuals was a lot different than reading a novel or short story. You had to read manuals very slowly to fully understand. No matter how fast a reader you were, technical manuals were a great equalizer. I liked electronics because of this. For the first time I was on an even playing field. I could read just as slowly as the next guy.

As I approached graduation from junior high school my parents realized that I had reached a crossroad. I was not progressing satisfactorily in the pre-college academic curriculum offered at the high school nearest our home. I was growing increasingly frustrated at school and it was taking a toll on me and my parents. Fortunately, my father had recently served on a Pittsfield city commission responsible for designing and building a comprehensive high school on the opposite side of town, and he knew that electronics was one of the options taught at the new school. Because of my interest in building electronic kits he suggested that I enroll in the electronics program at the new high school. Electronics, like the Drafting Program and Automotive Shop offered at the new high school, was for vocational kids. At that time vocational kids were thought of as students with inferior brain power and motivation. I somewhat reluctantly agreed to enroll in the Electronics Program. I was embarrassed to be enrolled in a vocational program but at least I could still play in the rock and roll band.

A few weeks after the fall semester began, the new school invited parents of the vocational students to tour the new vocational shop facilities and meet the teachers. My father accepted the invitation and duly met my electronics instructor. "Sir," said my teacher, "your son is a naturally gifted student. He has an almost intuitive sense of what happens in electronic equipment."

My father, who was then a member of the Pittsfield School Board, thought to himself, "You have to be kidding me." As it turned out the teacher was closer to the truth than my father imagined. I did have an excellent sense of electronics. By the end of the semester I began to blossom. I had found my metier.

I was lucky to have a natural sense of experimentation. I'd experiment by establishing a control group which was untouched by the experimental variable. Then I would compare it with an identical setup in which I changed variables. To aid my experimentation at home, I made a HeathKit oscilloscope, a power supply, a frequency generator, ohmmeter, etc, and I acquired quite a bit of other electronic test equipment by scrounging. I kept most of this electronic equipment in my bedroom.

One day there was a knock on my bedroom door. A couple visiting my parents came in. I will never forget their looks of astonishment. On my corner desk and shelves I was conducting an experiment on the effects of electromagnetic waves on the acceleration of cellular growth. I had a dozen avocado plants growing from seeds; I had suspended them in glasses of water using toothpicks. Six of the plants, a foot tall, were control plants. But the six plants in the experimental group had wires wrapped all the way up their stems, with the wires attached to a voltage generator and a flashing oscilloscope. I'm sure it looked bizarre. The experimental group were much larger in size than the control group. My visitors asked what it was all about. I told them the electromagnetic current was speeding the growth of the experimental group. I explained that I had created iron-enriched water for the experimental plants by adding iron filings to their water (I erroneously thought the electromagnetic waves were force-feeding nutrients up the stems, causing more rapid growth). The visitors were highly complimentary when they left. Twelve years later I turned on the TV and saw a special program announcing a startling new discovery. Scientists said that when bean plants were stimulated by an electromagnetic wave, their growth rate was drastically accelerated. I thought to myself, "Been there, done that." It was good to hear the reporter say that the scientists didn't know exactly why. My later-on-in-life guess is that when cells duplicate, they polarize. The polarization is normally created by micro, micro, pico voltages produced by the cell itself. This polarization can be induced artificially by electromagnetic waves. Perhaps this is the answer, perhaps it's just another wild guess. This was only one of many experiments I carried out in my bedroom.

In our electronics class we often got donations of large electronic modules from General Electric and other companies. What the class could not use after disassembly usually ended up in the garbage behind the school. I'd take my father's car and retrieve these things—bringing them home to our basement. One of my prize finds was a display module from an ABM missile launcher. The module, when energized, lit up like a Christmas tree in the dim basement. This "monster of doom" looked very pretty with all its colorful yellow, red and green pilot lights. It was difficult not to stare in wonder at the switch that read "FIRE." Right next to it was the switch that read "STANDBY." It made me wonder whether someone could accidentally fire a missile instead of *standing by* for further instructions. Visitors to our basement said it looked like a mad scientist's laboratory.

While working with electronic circuits I would often receive teeth-jarring shocks by accidentally touching a charged capacitor. Capacitors are electrical components which have the ability to store high voltages. Although the circuit containing the capacitor might be unplugged, electrical energy can still lurk in the capacitors. The shocks I received were painful, not only due to the actual electrical shock, but also due to the knee-jerk reaction that followed. I sometimes cut my hand or hit my head a painful knock when I was caught unaware by stored energy in a capacitor. We were taught in school to minimize the chance of receiving a bad shock by always keeping one hand in our pocket while probing a circuit with the other hand. This precluded taking a shock directly across the heart. Even with this precaution it sometimes hurt like hell when the probing hand got into high voltage territory.

My interest in all things electrical at this time got me into another scrape. The Methodist church our family attended had a youth fellowship which met every Sunday evening. We split into subgroups who took turns leading the program. When our turn came, the predetermined topic was "messages from God." At the end of the fellowship meeting, the young people stood around in a circle holding each other's hands while someone said the closing prayer.

I made a miniature shocking device out of a speaker transformer, a 9-volt battery and a micro-switch. While everyone had their heads bowed I took the device out of my pocket and had the people to the right and left of me each hold onto one of the wires. When the prayer came to the part "and you will feel God speak to you," I pressed the switch. Nothing happened. Everyone continued to hold hands. I pressed the button many times in rapid succession and the whole group threw their hands into the air. Apparently they thought the first shock was a signal from God. The next four or five they knew it was not! Boy, did I get in trouble that time. I was reprimanded and grounded for two weeks.

My high school curriculum was not composed entirely of electronics courses, though I would have liked that. I also had to endure English studies. Once in 12th grade I was sitting in an English class surrounded by my fellow looked-down-upon vocational kids. I was rocking on my chair in the last row, daydreaming about who knows what. The subject matter was an American classic titled "Spotted Horses." It was one of those trilaginous stories, written on one level with meanings that extended to many levels.

The teacher awakened me from my daydream by asking me to stand up and tell the class how I had interpreted the story. My brother, Richard, was going to Phillips Exeter Academy at the time and was an avid reader. He and I had discussed "Spotted Horses," so I was a little more prepared than usual. I stood up and answered rather slowly, "I think it is a fine example of how ontogeny recapitulates phylogeny."

The teacher's mouth dropped open; the class fell silent. After a long pause, the teacher asked, "Would you please repeat that?" I repeated what I had said. He gazed around the room as if he thought perhaps I had memorized those words without understanding their meaning. After all, I was just another vocational kid with a black leather jacket, sitting in the last row of his babysitting class. He grinned and asked, "Would you please explain to the rest of the class what you mean by those words?"

I answered, "I felt that the short story was a perfect example of how the personal development of an individual, or individuals in this case, paralleled the development of a larger group, for instance, a society." He asked to see me after class.

After the rest of the students had left he asked, "Clement, what the hell are you doing in this class?"

I replied, "I'm growing a fondness for American literature."

He chuckled and said, "I think you ought to try out for our school play because you are one hell of an actor. Now get out of here." He treated me with a little more respect after that day.

Extracurricular Things

When I reached the age of 15 my brother and I developed a passion for motorcycles. I mean *big-time* passion. We wanted to own one so badly. My parents said, "No motorcycles in this family...too dangerous!" So I did what any normal kid would do if he could: I bought a Honda 160 and kept it at a friend's house. It was a short ride through his backyard to the trails that wound all over the mountains and fields.

I spent many happy hours speeding over those dirt trails. A friend, who worked for the local power company, told me years later of seeing me from a power pole where he was working as I raced on cleared land under the power lines. It was great! I had lots of near misses but always seemed to escape disaster...until one day I came to a field with a huge mound of dirt. I thought if I was going fast enough I could climb over the dirt pile, so I *floored* it. I went right up the side at great speed. Once I cleared the top the source of the mound of dirt became apparent. It was excavated dirt from a basement of a house. The builder had dug 10 feet into the ground and piled the dirt up all around the hole. The height differential was a good 18 feet. There was no way to stop. I went down the other side of the mound of dirt and straight into the 10-foot basement excavation. The motorcycle cracked up and I lay in a heap...no broken bones, just a little blood from scrapes here and there. Not wanting to move, I lay there for a few minutes. There was absolutely no way to get the bike out. I finally collected myself, crawled out of the foundation and walked home. The next day when I went to inspect the bike, I found that the builder had kindly removed the motorcycle from his basement and set it on its side near a tree. The bike never worked after that.

Richard and I somehow talked our parents into letting us get three-wheelers. They were small low-rider trail buggies with gasoline engines and centripetal clutches. Because of their small size, my parents were lulled into the belief we would not be at risk in riding them. Wrong! Where there is a will there is a way. We found risks by looking for risks.

Richard was an indifferent mechanic. He was riding down a trail in front of me one day when all of a sudden my throttle broke and I went to full speed with no way to slow down. To avoid crashing into him, I steered around him and passed him in a flash. Across the trail was a tree put there to keep vehicles from driving up the mountain. Seeing the tree, I turned my body around and depressed the kill-switch, a piece of metal that grounded the spark plug directly to the engine block to short out the spark plug and *kill* the engine. When I did, I received a jolt of electricity so I had to let go of the kill-switch. The vehicle was still going full speed toward the tree that blocked the trail. Before I crashed into the tree I rolled off the vehicle and the left wheel ran over my shoulder and down my back. As I slid along the path to a halt, I watched the three-wheeler run off the side of the path and flip over.

My brother drove up not knowing the technical difficulty I experienced and asked, "What are you doing? What did you do that for?"

I told him, "The throttle broke and stuck on full blast. I couldn't slow down or stop, so I bailed!"

We turned the vehicle back upright and he acted like he was fixing it. He moved some things this way and that way and then declared, "There, I've fixed it."

I sat in the seat as he pulled the cord to start the engine. The second he did the thing bolted forward like a shot. He hadn't fixed anything. Actually, he had no idea what was wrong. Again I rolled off the vehicle but this time when it flipped, my three-wheeler got a badly bent front wheel, the engine cover and seat flew off and the carburetor ended up somewhere in the woods. Richard, I'll get you back some day, you crazy brother! But it wasn't really his fault. Three-wheelers can be dangerous and if you choose to ride them the way we did, accidents are bound to happen. I once saw Richard driving across a gravel pit when his brake cable broke and wrapped around his rear wheel. He flipped, landing on his head. Kids—*don't try this at home!*

One summer, during my high school years, I worked as a nature counselor for a local day camp. It was tucked away in a beautiful mountain setting and owned by a lawyer, Rudy Sacco. Rudy loved children. As a nature counselor I took the children on nature walks and pointed out the many beauties along the trails, some of which were difficult to see.

At the camp there was a building with many cages and aquariums that housed various animals, reptiles and bugs that we caught and held captive until the end of the week when they were set free. One of the favorite activities, which the children also enjoyed, was to catch bugs and feed them to the ever-hungry bats, praying mantises and toads in the display cages. Mice were always plentiful and fun to watch because they were always active.

At the end of one long day, as I was locking up the nature building, I chanced to turn my head toward the main house. I noticed that the chain link gate to the swimming pool, which was located beyond the main house, was moving. Jerry, the five-year-old son of the maintenance man, was squeezing his way through the locked gate of the 10-foot fence that surrounded the pool.

I ran up the driveway as fast as I could toward the pool. Jerry got through the space between the gate and fence, walked over to the deep end of the pool and started swishing the water with his hands. He fell in fully clothed. I was at a full run. Jerry splashed around in panic. I reached the gate but could not fit through the gap, so I climbed up the side of the 10-foot fence using my fingers and toes. I dropped down to the concrete on the other side and ran over to where Jerry was struggling. He had tired and gone under. I knelt down, grabbed him by his collar and pulled him out onto the concrete slab. Gurgling water, Jerry coughed. He had no idea that he was given a second chance at life. I looked around and there was no one else in sight.

Years later when I worked as a suicide counselor for an emergency 800 Hot Line, the memory of Jerry falling in the pool would come back and give me strength. Having suicidal thoughts is like falling in a deep pool of water with no one around. You feel lonely and grow weary of struggling. All it takes is one person to save you—not two or more. Just one person who perceives the trouble you are in and reaches to pull you back to safety. If you ever find yourself in this kind of trouble, yell for help. There are many lifeguards out there.

Rudy Sacco had lots of influential friends. After I had worked at his day camp he found a job for me working for the State Highway

Department. He also got jobs for other people. Another person Rudy helped was Mark, a Vietnam vet. After risking his life during two tours in 'Nam, Mark came home and couldn't find employment until he met Rudy.

Our work crew had large vehicles designed for cutting and hauling large trees that might fall on electrical lines or motorists. One lunch break I was squatting near a brook observing little fish scurrying about when I heard Mark and another buddy approach. Mark asked, "Tom, are you by chance Korean?"

I looked surprised and blurted, "No, I'm from Pittsfield."

Mark was an amateur psychologist. He looked into the brook at the fish and said, "By the way you were squatting, I thought you might have come from Korea. In 'Nam, if there were quite a few of us Green Beret and Special Forces troops walking down a sidewalk and there were two Korean soldiers walking toward us, we'd all get off the sidewalk and let the Korean soldiers by. The word among us was "You can mess with some people, but not with them."

I answered, "I'm Korean!"

Snow skiing is one of my favorite sports. Lucky for me, Pittsfield, where we lived, was in the Berkshire Mountains which provided ample opportunity to ski. Our family had a season's pass to a local ski resort with a rope tow so skiing was a recreation we could all do together. I started skiing at an early age. By the time I was in high school I had skill plus a maniacal approach to down-hilling.

I skied on a high school team one winter as a down-hiller. My favorite style was to get into a "racing tuck" and hold it no matter how painful it got. We called it *thigh burn*. One day on the ski slopes the coach asked me to try jumping because he had noted that I liked to do "spread eagles," "tip-ups," and the like. The other members of the jumping team were there and had already made their practice jumps.

The coach instructed me, "Tom, the first time you go over the jump, don't jump. Just relax and keep your balance. The jumping will come later. I just want to see how you look and handle yourself in the air." Simple enough. I walked up to the top of the short run and prepared for take-off. The coach and other team members stood to one side of the jump. One of the members was a young lady by the name of Sarah. She was cute. She had the kind of smile that could brighten a dimly lit room.

I made up my mind that on the first try I was not going to follow the coach's instructions. I was going to impress the whole team, the coach and especially Sarah! I was going to do the world's longest, highest jump ever seen! I pushed off and got into a racing tuck which was not on the agenda. At high speed I approached the jump and when the skis hit the jump and were about to leave the snow, I straightened my legs out and jumped as high into the air as I could. It was a great jump. My body lifted vertically and horizontally, passing the snow marks where previous jumpers had landed. However, due to my inexperience, my body started to rotate forward ever so slowly. I could not keep from rotating more and more forward as I was approaching the ground.

The first thing that made contact were the tips of the skis, jabbing straight into the snow and snapping both tips off. The first part of my body that hit the ground was my chest, followed by a whiplash landing on my face. I did not slide; I stopped abruptly with the broken tips of my skis anchored in the ground. I never lost consciousness. The coach, the students and Sarah came running. I couldn't get that first breath of air. I fought and fought and just could not inhale air. It seemed like forever before I could finally breathe. Boy, were they impressed. They were impressed that I lived! They were impressed that I only broke a couple of ribs. Sarah told me later, "Your face turned the prettiest robin's egg blue that I have ever seen."

Thirty years after my "long jump" on skis I was invited by Dr. H. Peter Doble, II to ski with him and his friends and family at Sun Valley, Idaho. Dr. Doble is President of the Western Institute for Surgical Education in Twin Falls, Idaho. At the institute they train surgeons from all over the world in the techniques of powered endoscopic sinus surgery. I explained to Dr. Doble before arriving that I was rusty since I had lived in Indiana for a long time and hadn't had much opportunity to ski for over a decade. Out of concern for my safety he engaged an instructor to ski with me the first day. When the instructor and I got to the top of the mountain, the instructor told me to go ahead of him so he could observe me as I descended. I started out tentatively but soon felt myself recovering my old form. I went

Skiing Sun Valley, Idaho with Dr. Peter Doble

into a racing tuck and let it all hang out. When we reached the bottom of the mountain the instructor said, "Tom, you don't need me to teach you to ski." He started to walk away, then turned and said, "As a matter of fact, skiing with you scares me to death." I am not suicidal...accident-prone maybe, but definitely not suicidal.

One weekend my family went to Vermont to ski on a real ski slope with a chair lift and long trails. My sister Leslie was not happy about the weekend agenda and complained about the long car ride, the cold when we got there and the fact that she wouldn't have anybody her age to ski with on the beginner's slope. We got to the ticket booth and Leslie fell down. She said, "I think I broke my arm."

My dad said, "You didn't break your arm and you are going skiing with the rest of us." Minutes later it became apparent that Leslie *had* broken her arm...end of weekend!

A couple of years later we were at a Strawberry Festival

luncheon at North River fire station in the Adirondack Mountains. Leslie was outside playing with other children while my parents sat inside the fire station eating strawberry shortcake and visiting with friends. Leslie attempted to balance herself on top of a upended picnic table and failed on the dismount. She walked into the fire station and announced, "I think I broke my other arm." There was no argument this time. We went directly to the local doctor...end of another weekend!

All-American Family

My family in America was not like the Waltons on TV. Each of us seemed to have strong motivations to do things but not always in the same direction. My mother had received a very liberal education at Smith College in Massachusetts. Her favorite activities revolved around the United Nations and liberal causes of every persuasion. My father was a conservative businessman and worked extremely hard for the General Electric Company, first as an engineer and then as a manufacturing executive. My siblings and I were all strong-willed and intent on doing *our own thing*...in my sister Carolyn's words spoken as a small child, "By myself!" My mother used to lament, "Why couldn't I have been given at least one easy child!"

Guiding their four children was not easy for my parents. In addition to the usual problems of shepherding children through childhood, parents of the sixties and seventies had to deal with the political fallout of the Vietnam War, the sexual revolution, the rise of the feminist movement and many other generational changes. Children were encouraged by their teachers and the media to challenge everything that age and authority espoused.

"Don't trust anybody over thirty," young people in America cried. Except me! I was a rock-solid conservative. I didn't have any sympathy with the young American student rebels marauding across their campuses. I might have been conservative by nature. Or perhaps it was the result of my deprivation in Korea.

An elderly man said to me, "You and I have a different perspective on life because I grew up during the Great Depression."

I replied, "Quite to the contrary, I also grew up during very hard economic times. You and I have very similar outlooks."

My mother would take us children to her mother's summer cottage in the Adirondack Mountains for part of each summer. The cottage was situated on several acres of cleared land in the town of North River. Actually, "town" is not very accurate. "Crossroads" would be a more appropriate description. In addition to a few houses, there was a small convenience store run by Willard (still is) and a gas station. The only building of any size, a small hotel, burned to the ground in what was suspected to be an act of an arsonist who torched a number of Adirondack buildings during the 1950s and 1960s.

We kids had a number of activities to occupy our time at our summer retreat. Swimming at Thirteenth Lake was a regular activity. The cottage we lived in was dependent on a shallow well for water and luxuries like an indoor bathtub and toilet were not possible. My earliest memories are of using a hand pump at the kitchen sink to get water for cooking and washing our hands. I remember that we had to go to a nearby farm to get ice for an old-fashioned icebox we had in our kitchen. The farmer, Mr. Cleveland, cut ice at Thirteenth Lake during the winter and stored it in a small icehouse with sawdust covering the ice. Mr. Cleveland was retired by this time and his land had gone back to trees. He told us that the wooded hillsides visible from our cottage were all cleared farmland when he was a boy. He told of once walking to Wevertown, 14 miles distant, and back to get a sack of corn milled so he could bake johnnycake. He carried the sack of corn all that way.

My mother used to pay us kids a penny for each small evergreen tree we pulled from our summer property. We protested that this was too little pay but in one summer we completely cleared a two-acre field behind our cottage of the intruding trees.

For several summers this field was home to Ruggles, a swayback horse our mother had bought to ride. She dearly loved that horse and it was quite handsome when my mother filled the gap in the horse's back. She once went riding in Pittsfield and proudly told us when she returned that a stranger had asked her if Ruggles was a thoroughbred racehorse. My father was skeptical of Ruggles' ancestry and maintained that the horse lacked "smarts." His belief in this regard was confirmed when he attempted to ride Ruggles from our home to the barn some two miles distant. He let Ruggles choose the path through the woods leading to the barn and relied on the old saying that an animal knows by instinct how best to get home. When the horse took them into a swampy area, my father kept assuring himself that the animal knew best. Wrong! Ruggles got so mired in the wet ground that he eventually fell on his side with a sigh, pitching my father into the muck. Boy, what Dad said about that horse!

When we got dirty while at our summer place my father would take Richard and me for a bath in Thirteenth Brook. The water was crystal clear and ice-cold. Dad would make us use plenty of soap and scrub until we shone. It was such a delicious feeling to put on warm, clean clothes when Dad said we were sufficiently clean.

Richard and I got a memorable swimming lesson from Dad in Thirteenth Lake. Richard and I were on the lake with him in a boat and we boys jumped in for a swim. Dad suggested that we attempt to swim clear across the lake, something that seemed entirely beyond our capability. He said, "I will stay only the length of an oar from you and can give you an oar to grasp anytime you insist that you have reached your limit." We protested…swam, protested some more and eventually reached the other side of the lake without assistance.

My parents tried to instill in their children a strong sense of obligation toward others. We went regularly to church, and my parents' church and community activities were a constant example for us of how adults should act. At our home in Pittsfield on Sundays there was a ritual of sorts in my family. First there was church. My mother ran late for everything and it was always difficult to get six people fed and dressed on Sunday morning fast enough to get to church service on time. The church choir could have set their watches by the regular spectacle of the Clement family slipping into the church balcony fifteen minutes late. The only instance I can recall that we might have made it to church on time was scotched when my sister Leslie, age four, discovered that she did not have underpants on under her dress. She found this half-way to church and we lost our chance to be on time by going back for the underpants.

After we got back home from church on Sundays we engaged in another part of our Sunday ritual: Cleanup! My father would survey the piles of schoolbooks, hockey sticks, baseball gloves, etc. that we kids had left sitting on the floor, stairs and other flat places…plus the piles of petitions my mother had accumulated in her various crusades to make the earth a better place to live. He'd declare, "Nobody is going anywhere or doing anything until this place is cleaned up!" Thereupon, we would each tackle a different room, making abundant use of available closets to hide our *stuff*. When the house looked sufficiently presentable, my father would sit down to read the Sunday paper and the rest of us got on with our lives. Of course, by Monday evening everything came out of the closets and confusion reigned again. My mother extended her charitable work to include our cleaning lady, who once a week tried to put the Clement house in order. For a number of years our designated cleaning lady was a single woman who had the habit of getting pregnant by various men, that is until my mother took her to New York State where it was legal to prescribe birth control diaphragms. Until this remedy was found, my father complained that we were the only house in town cleaned by someone suffering from perpetual morning sickness.

Transporting four children to various extracurricular activities was a formidable exercise for my parents when we children were very young. Some relief came with our arrival at puberty, though it was accompanied by a new set of problems. Before children learn to drive, parents are aware of the child's travel destination. This is not to say that said transported child stays at said destination. In the case of my siblings and me this was indeed not certain. But once we started driving a car, the task of parenting became considerably more difficult. This was and is very common in American middle-class life.

I recall one warm summer evening my father was reading the evening newspaper when a neighbor boy, Timmy, opened our front screen door and asked my father where I was. "Oh," said my father, "he is spending the night at Larry's."

"Thank you," said Timmy and he left.

Five minutes later my brother, Richard, walked in from outside. My father asked him where he had been and Richard said, "Out."

Then my sister, Leslie, came in from outside and, when asked by my father where she had been, she answered, "Out."

In the meantime, I wasn't at Larry's house with Larry. Larry and I had gone to spend the night at Greg's house because his parents were away and that had certain advantages. Greg, Larry and I had gone several blocks away to the home of Greg's girlfriend where a girls' slumber party was in progress. We three boys were on a shed roof at the rear of the house where the slumber party was, trying to persuade the girls to come out of the house, when word reached us that another friend of ours, Alan, had driven up the hill past my parents' house to where the pavement ended and was stuck in the mud. The fact that he had his girlfriend with him made the matter too delicate to mention to a parent, so we were asked to hurry quietly therewith to the rescue of said Alan and female friend. That was why Timmy had asked my dad earlier, "Where's Tom?" Alan had asked Timmy to go to my house and ask me to bring a shovel up the hill to help Alan get out of the mud. Richard and Leslie knew of the youthful *Mayday* when they walked into our living room and said they had been out. Actually, they were headed upstairs to try to telephone me, Mr. Fixit, at Larry's.

Anyhow, after we managed to extract Alan's car from the mud, I walked into our house with Larry and Greg to wash our hands and use the bathroom. When we left, my father asked me where we were headed and I made the mistake of saying as I went out the front door, "Out."

My father folded his newspaper and walked out onto our front porch where he announced loudly to all within earshot, "I don't believe a darn word any of you say." He then went back inside and resumed reading his newspaper. When my father reads this, thirty years later, he will know he was right: you couldn't believe a darn thing we said on warm summer nights when our hormones were raging.

Slings and Arrows

Throughout my childhood in America, I was periodically subjected to ridicule by both children and grown-ups. One day I was awaiting my mother after a trumpet lesson when two boys a little older than me came by, shoved me to the ground, and kicked me over and over, saying "Hey Chink, where'd you get those funny eyes? Ha ha ha...you little twerp."

When my mother arrived she could tell I had been in some kind of scuffle. When she asked me what happened, I could only sob. I could never say, "Some prejudiced boys beat me up and called me a Chink." Perhaps she knew anyway. There was nothing I could do at the time. We lived in a predominantly white city with few black people and even fewer Asians. My hope was to someday grow up big and strong and be able to take care of myself...and five or six others!

Although most of the people around me accepted and befriended me in America, it seemed I would always be reminded of my "differentness." What is it in people that makes them feel so afraid of others different than themselves? I have lived with Korean people, American Caucasian people, American Black people and German people. They all sleep, eat, laugh, cry and die. They all need the same things from friends, family and the world.

I had my share of girlfriends while growing up. The girls usually were unaffected by my being biracial but I got some interesting reactions from their parents.

In the U.S. it is usual for parents to want their offspring to date and eventually marry people of the same race and religion. "Please find a nice Jewish boy...girl" (or Italian, or Irish, etc.) is the usual plea of parents to a daughter or son in America. When I entered, "Who," they asked themselves, "is this?" I certainly wasn't Jewish or Italian or Irish. For Caucasian Americans I sometimes wasn't Caucasian enough. And, for Asiatic Americans I sometimes wasn't Asian enough.

I had a girlfriend who was all Korean. Her name was Marisa. Marisa's parents were straight from Korea. Her father worked as an engineer for an international company. Her grandmother lived in the same house with them. That is a wonderful Korean custom—taking in elderly relatives. I was in love with Marisa and I very much wanted to learn the Korean language, both to speak and write it. She started giving me lessons. I knew I would learn very quickly as it was already in my past...in my blood.

One day her mother took me aside and said, "You only be friends with Marisa, okay? No marriage. Only friend." I was crushed. I knew it was because I was half-and-half. I thought perhaps to a Korean family living here in the U.S. it wouldn't matter. Well, it did. They were from the old school of thought. It was fine if Marisa married a 100% white man. That would not be a disgrace to her family. What was I to do? I did not choose to be half-and-half; it was my fate. I understand history and I know that Koreans consider it important to have a purebred nation. Perhaps someday they can find it in their hearts to accept both sides of me.

I once was invited to a Caucasian girl's house for dinner and all her mother said during the entire meal was, "I like rice" to which I replied, "That's nice," and later, "I know how to use chop sticks too" to which I said, "That's nice too."

I had a girlfriend with whom I had a very close relationship until the subject of religion came up. We got into an argument with her mother over going to church one Sunday, and the mother turned to me and said, "You represent the *dark forces*." I am not sure whether she was referring to the color of my skin or that I was in league with the devil, Beelzebub!

When I meet new people, my part-Asian appearance can elicit strange responses. I met a group of people who didn't often meet foreigners. One guy shook my hand and said, "Why, you don't speak English too bad!"

Shaking his hand, I replied, "Why, you don't speak too badly yourself, buddy! But if you don't mind me saying so, I think you meant to say badly." He was surprised. It's funny how outward appearances can fool you. "You can't judge a book by the cover...."

I especially enjoy people who give me a suspicious stare before saying, "What are you anyway? I know you're something."

Usually I respond, "I am an alien and have proof," referring to my immigration papers which state in black and white that I am indeed an alien. They could have been a little more specific about my origin. The cosmos is such a large place and they didn't even specify which galaxy. What if I wanted to return home some day? How would I even know which direction to take? I never have found the crash site of my saucer. But with my technical skills, I'm 100% confident that it would soon be running once again. In any case, I promise never to fly over Roswell again.

Junior College

After I graduated from Taconic High School I went on to junior college. My first college was Berkshire Community College located in Pittsfield. The Electrical Engineering Program there was much different than the Electronics Vocational Program at high school. Instead of being looked upon as lesser human beings, engineering students were looked upon as eggheads with pocket protectors and calculators swinging from their belt loops. After receiving my first semester final grades I had my first inkling that perhaps I wasn't as dumb as I always thought I was. My report card contained all A's and B's.

One of the required courses was sociology. This class went on a couple of field trips. The first field trip the class took was to a public housing project in Springfield, Massachusetts. The project was very rundown and looked like a war zone. The lower apartments were all boarded up with plywood covered with graffiti. The upper floors were reached by elevator. When the elevator doors opened the smell of urine was strong enough to make your eyes burn. The elevator floor was a mess, as were the hall floors and, probably, the apartment interiors. As our bus pulled out of the trash-covered, blacktop parking lot, which was painted green to look like grass, I couldn't help thinking how fortunate I was. Why had I escaped poverty and the people here had not? The experience left me troubled, which was probably the purpose of the college-sponsored field trips.

The second field trip the class took was to North Hampton Mental Institution, a state-run institution. When we arrived we walked in single file through armed, locked gates on various floors of the wards. In one large room, as we walked by patients who were extremely disturbed, a woman left her place near a wall, walked right up to me, grabbed my arm, tugged fiercely and yelled, "I want this one. This is the one I want. This one is mine!" Two aides had to run over to set me free. The class thought it was funny. I felt sorry for her.

We went to another floor and there was *Harold*. Two years previous I had met him in the Pittsfield teenage social scene. His father was a judge in a nearby town and Harold seemed very confident and outgoing. But then he dropped out of the social scene and no one heard from him. He now wore a white T-shirt and was playing pool with another patient. He came up to me and said, "Hi Tom, can I have a piece of gum? They won't let us chew gum around here because they think we'll choke on it, stick it to some furniture, or put it in someone's hair. How's it goin'?"

I was perplexed. What was Harold doing here? Was life that unmanageable that what appeared to me a perfectly normal guy had to be placed in a mental institution? I gave him some gum and talked with him for awhile. He seemed perfectly normal to me, exactly as he did in the outside world.

It was not until a few years later I realized he might have dodged the Vietnam draft by checking into the mental health facility. Perhaps he thought it was preferable to risk one's sanity rather than lose one's life in the jungles of a strange land.

For a time I worked as an aide in a home for mentally challenged children. The children had a variety of disabilities...hyperactive, Mongoloid, autistic and violent. I am lucky in that there has always been and will always be a little boy in me. Children perceive this immediately. We bond upon first contact. I am not a chastising parent, one that frowns and punishes. I am a huge kid with money and a car. Watch out!!! My brother Richard came from the University of Massachusetts one day to visit me and have lunch at the children's home. One of the Mongoloid kids made him laugh at the table. Another child who was classified as mentally handicapped said to my brother, "You shouldn't laugh. Someday when you are old, you will be just like him." That certainly made my brother stop and think.

I grew to love those children. The experiences they shared with me have been some of the greatest gifts on earth. One of the things I learned while working with them is that it's the commonality of individuals that brings people together. If there is no commonality, there is no friendship. A "well-adjusted person" will have a multitude of commonalties with a multitude of friends. The more well-adjusted you are, the more friends you have, the more people can relate to you. Many mentally challenged children, on the other hand, do not have the ability to have more than one or two friends. Many have a "best friend." If they meet another potential friend they must terminate the first relationship and develop another one-on-one friendship. Think about this: when non-mentally challenged children are developing social habits, it is not uncommon that they also have very few best friends. They then go through a "falling out" with these friends before developing new ones. We see this every day. As an individual grows older and more well-adjusted he should also develop the capacity to avoid "trashing" old friends for new ones. Perhaps everyone could acquire such gifts by paying attention and giving themselves to unfortunate people, rather than ignoring them or treating them as outcasts of society. Perhaps we all might grow to be more well-adjusted and have a larger circle of friendship without trashing one for the other. It may be a little painful at first, but the rewards are immeasurable and we will have a special place in heaven. I know these special children do.

Although I stayed in the electronics program for two years, my interest in electronics was overridden by a desire to study psychology and work with troubled children and adults. I went to Austen Riggs, a mental health facility in Stockbridge, Massachusetts, for an interview to work as an aide. There were many prominent people working there, some of whom had written important books on psychology: Eric Fromm, Eric Erickson, and Eleanor Gibson. Mrs. Gibson was the mother of my good friend, Tom Gibson, who was one of the most incredible drummers I have had the pleasure of hearing. Tom's father, William Gibson, wrote *The Miracle Worker*, the Helen Keller story. Tom and I used to play rock and roll music by the hour.

Many famous people went to Austen Riggs. Jim Morrison took refuge there for a period of time. It is a world-renowned facility with premier psychiatrists and psychologists. I didn't get hired…never made it past the first interview. During lunch with the interviewer a white Cadillac limousine zoomed up the circular drive in front of the ivory-pillared building where we sat. The car door was flung open and a young lady waltzed out, leaving her door ajar. She came into the cafeteria, cut in line, grabbed some food and sat down next to me.

The interviewer said to her, "Carol, do you think that is an appropriate place to park and appropriate behavior in the cafeteria?"

Carol answered, "Fuck off, bitch, I can park wherever the hell I want to!" and continued to eat. I would have just loved to have worked there.

A very sad thing happened when I was 21. My mother fell ill and her doctors were not able to determine the cause. She underwent exploratory surgery and it was thought that the problem was fixed. It had to do with her pancreas. Several months later she had a relapse and had to be taken to Boston for another operation by a specialist. This time the verdict was incurable cancer. She lingered for several months at Pittsfield General Hospital, where we visited her daily. Toward the end, I was sitting with my mother. She was trying to eat a bowl of soup, but couldn't because she was doubled over with stomach pain. I put my arms around her and said, "Mom, make yourself eat. You *have* to force yourself to eat."

She looked at me with an expression that told me that she knew and I knew that it was almost over. She took my hand and said, "Thomas, you think too much. Don't think so much. I am very proud of you. You are in college and your grades are good. I knew you could make it. Don't think so much. I love you." She died a week later.

That night as our family sat down to dinner without her, grief overwhelmed me. I did not want to cry in front of the rest of the family. When I got up to leave, my father asked me to stay and tried to console me. The other kids told him to let me go. I ran up the mountain where there was a little waterfall, knelt down next to a white birch tree and cried. I still miss her. I always will.

My mother made it her personal project to get me to America. She made sure I studied and did my homework before I watched TV or went out to play. She was constantly on a mission to help me learn and get accepted. I don't think she would have ever imagined what the future held in store for me. I know she's smiling down at me from above. I am forever grateful and will always love her.

My interest in electronics was waning. I read one psychology book after another and was not studying my major. In computer class the teacher showed everyone how to use a slide rule. He noticed I was gazing out the window and said, "OK Tom, show us all what the square root of 30 is."

I thought about it for a moment, knowing that in my head I could easily figure out the first two or three digits. Yet I knew that with a slide rule you could go to three or four digits beyond the decimal point. I blurted, "It's 5.477." As it turned out, it was a very good guess. The instructor asked to see me after class.

After class he said, "Tell me how you did that." I just shrugged my shoulders. "How in the world did you get the number correct to three decimal points without using a slide rule? Why aren't you doing better in this class, Tom? Have you lost interest? You have such potential but you are not applying yourself. I know you have just lost your mother. Would you like to speak with the school counselor? It may help you."

I didn't want to *speak* with the school counselor. I wanted to *be* the school counselor. I wanted to study psychology. As far as guessing the answer to the math problem was concerned, I didn't profess to be some kind of math whiz. But I thought the first digit in the answer was obvious. The next three were a lucky guess. It sure confused the hell out of the computer teacher though! He thought I was a little Einstein walking around in clouds thinking up some theory of relativity. The only theory I could come up with was *mind over matter. If you don't mind...it doesn't matter.*

At the end of the second year of junior college, I did change my major to psychology, much to the dismay of my father, the electrical engineer. I was not alone in wanting to study psychology. Interest in psychology was very high among college students at that time. Americans were doing a lot of soul-searching because of the Vietnam war and the loss of confidence in government, including the military. There was a general unease that we were going down the wrong path as a nation. Among college kids the talk was of "getting your head straight." Maybe I wanted to get my head straight.

Studying psychology was fascinating. I took a class in Experimental Psychology taught by Professor Woody Prince. One day Professor Prince demonstrated ESP cards in front of a large auditorium audience. He talked about ESP and said some people could tell what the cards were by thought alone. It seemed pretty farfetched to me.

There were six different cards, so there was one chance in six of being right by simply guessing. He held up a card so no one could see it. Everyone fell silent. I spoke up, "It's the wavy lines." He turned the card around and sure as heck it was the wavy lines. The audience applauded. He shuffled the deck, pulled up another card and held it high. I blurted, "It's the positive symbol." He turned it around and it was the positive symbol. The class cheered. Mr. Prince wanted a third try, but I quit. I thought, "Why ruin a perfect record?" Professor Prince made me feel really good about myself. He said that I was way above average intelligence and that I should go to a facility in West Virginia which had electronic means of measuring intelligence. It measured brain waves as pictures were flashed at high speeds in front of you. I always wanted to do that but never did. The ESP cards were a lucky guess. There were only six different symbols so the chances were pretty good of guessing one of them correctly. It was funny though, to guess two in a row correctly in front of the whole auditorium.

Professor Prince was a most exceptional teacher. He had a pilot's license and took a group of us in an airplane to run our personal experiments on weightlessness. We brought objects with us so we could experiment with a weightless environment during a free-fall in the plane. I brought up a ball, a rock, and a pencil. During the free fall I let go of the pencil and there it stayed, floating in front of my face. I hit the end of the pencil and it shot into my other hand like a bullet. The rock floated just as easily as the light ball and could be spun.

Back in the classroom, Professor Prince asked us to share our perceptions with the rest of the class. I was hesitant but he urged me to speak what was on my mind. I said, "It seems that on earth, with gravity as a force, everything becomes relative to the earth and everything on it is connected. In space, you become the center of your own consciousness. You are not connected to anything. You are the center of your own force." He smiled the widest grin ever. He liked that response.

While studying psychology in junior college I still gravitated toward my engineering friends. One day when I approached the lunchroom table where they were sitting, I could see merriment on their faces. When I got to the table I learned the source of their glee. Most guys think that their table-talk is too raunchy for the opposite sex. Well, my friends had concealed a miniature FM transmitter in a baseball cap which they had placed on a table frequented by female students. The girls were heard discussing the male students whom they observed in the lunchroom in terms that certainly rivaled anything the male students said at their tables. It was a revelation to me. Wow! XXXX

The U.S. was in the middle of the Vietnam War while I was in my second year of junior college. Students were rioting and getting shot at Kent State in Ohio; the Woodstock rock and roll festival was in full swing. U.S. society was going in several different directions at once. I felt the urge to go to Vietnam so I went into an Air Force recruiting office and took their electronics entry test. The officer there got extremely excited. He said, "You blew the top off that test, son! You could be an officer!" Arlo Guthrie's song "Alice's Restaurant" came to mind. The officer and I started to jump up and down yelling the line of "Alice's Restaurant," "I want to KEEEEL!...I want to KEEEEEEEL!!!" And then he blew it. He said, "I see you're from Korea. Why, you'll be going home!"

What! Korea?? Home??? I thought, "The U.S. is my home. Wait just a minute now." I had to think about these conflicting feelings for the first time in many years. It hurt. Home? I did come from Korea, didn't I? Maybe Korea really is my home? Where is home? Is home where you were born? Is home where you currently go to sleep? Is home where you keep all your *stuff*? I didn't know. But I couldn't get away from that recruiting officer fast enough. I said, "I want to go to Vietnam...not Korea." He hounded me for weeks after that. I don't think he ever realized the button he pushed. I never went into the Air Force. I played rock and roll.

I also got an opportunity to spend a semester studying in Germany. I had a wonderful opportunity to study physics, the German language and German literature at Bonn University in Germany. If you ever want to learn a language, go there. The country is one of the most beautiful ever! I walked in the Black Forest, where brooks full of trout meandered down the mountain. The Rhine River with castles overlooking the scenic view is breathtaking. The beer and wine are some of the best in the world.

I loved a custom which the Germans have in restaurants. In America, if you go to a restaurant, you find an empty table and perhaps sit alone to eat. In Germany it is customary that no matter how many empty tables there are you find an empty chair at a table already occupied and sit down with the people already eating. This promotes social behavior and conversation rather than eating in silence by yourself. In a store or pub, when a total stranger comes in they look right at you and say, "Gruss Gott." Translated, this means, "Greet God."

Their technology is superior to any I have seen. Would you rather drive a Mercedes or a Yugo? The Autobahn is an incredible experience. I was with German students driving 140 mph when a car came out of nowhere and passed us so fast that our car shook. They were gone in an instant!

I lived with a woman there for three months. Her father was a foreign diplomat. They didn't care that I was a Korean-American adoptee. They thought I was neat. We rode bikes through beautiful country mountains. If you ever want to visit a most beautiful country, go to Germany.

Indiana

After my mother passed away, my father left the General Electric Company. A neighbor, Howard Kaufman, was president of Kay Bee Toy & Hobby Shops, a small chain of retail stores in New England. My father and mother and Mr. and Mrs. Kaufman socialized together, and the Kaufman and Clement children played together. My father approached Mr. Kaufman regarding buying a franchise for one or more toy stores bearing the Kay Bee name. After discussing franchising, it was decided that it would be better to set up a separate corporation jointly owned by Kay Bee stockholders and my father, with an option to merge later. This was agreed to, with the Midwest designated as the area where the new corporation would operate. My father then moved to Indianapolis, Indiana, while I stayed in Pittsfield and lived at the High Point Art Gallery Inn with Doris Barden, a good friend of my family. The rooms there usually cost $65 per night; she let me stay for free. I mowed the lawn and did various chores which really didn't amount to much. Many well-known people visited the Gallery and Inn: William Shirer, author of *The Rise and Fall of the Third Reich*, William Gibson, author of *The Miracle Worker*, Simon and Garfunkel, Jim Morrison, Eric Fromm, Eric Erickson. The list goes on and on. Many famous people lived in or visited the Berkshire Mountains.

After graduating from Berkshire Community College, I moved to Indiana to live with my dad. The first time I drove from Massachusetts to Indiana I got lost as I was driving around looking for my father's new residence. I stopped at a gas station and asked, "Would you please help me? I am lost."

He answered, "You're not lost. You're right here." It may not seem like much, but as an adoptee, whenever I believe I am lost, I always remember his words, "You're not lost. You're right here."

In Indianapolis, I met Park Jung Jay, a Master in Tae Kwon Do (a form of Korean karate). He was my very first Korean friend. He is more kind than words can describe. He gave me Tae Kwon Do lessons for free because, as he put it, "Your name is Thomas *Park*

Clement (Park is like Smith in Korea). You may be my brother. Family members don't pay." He came to our house and cooked Korean food for us. It was the first time in a very long time that I had eaten Korean food. It was so delicious; I loved it. Besides Tae Kwon Do we did other things together, like going to music concerts at Butler University and playing volleyball, one of my favorite team sports. At the time I met Master Park, he and other Koreans were creating a Tae Kwon Do Federation in the United States. They had to choose a name, a logo and an acronym for their organization. Master Park called me one day and said, "We are going to call it the Korean Karate Kudokwon. It will be the KKK."

Respect for your Tae Kwon Do Master is a must. You should not even walk on the shadow of your Master. I had to be very careful in answering Master Park so as not to be disrespectful or appear arrogant. Carefully, I said, "Master Park, I think that is a wonderful idea. However, there already...is...a...small...klan of people in the United States who use the abbreviation KKK. I am very afraid that people may get our organization confused with this group." He took it very well. The Federation was not called the KKK. Thank God!

While living with my father in Indianapolis, I attended IUPUI, Indiana University-Purdue University Indianapolis. We lived in an apartment complex near 86th Street and Westfield Boulevard. It was there I met my best friend, Bob Berry. We both played guitar and were into Tae Kwon Do. We spent hours, days, weeks, months, and years together as friends. We had such great times together!

My father had a Kay Bee Toy and Hobby store in Indianapolis and Bob and I would go to the toy store and buy whatever we wanted with a family discount. One day we purchased a gas-powered helicopter. The directions said that it would fly straight up in the air until it ran out of gas and glide straight down to where it had taken off, landing gently without harm. We went out to the parking lot in front of our apartment and fired that baby up. It was getting to be dusk, so there wasn't a lot of light left in the day. The helicopter went straight up as the directions said. About 40 feet in the air, it slanted 45 degrees and took off horizontally, heading toward Indianapolis. We never saw it again. That was an expensive toy. I guess we didn't read the small print which must have said, "single use only."

Bob and I took Tae Kwon Do from Park Jung Jay for many years. We also had the incredible opportunity of taking lessons on Keystone Avenue at the Olympic Karate Studio. We were taught by Bill "Super Foot" Wallace, who held the world title in full contact TKO Tae Kwon Do until he quit to become Elvis Presley's bodyguard.

Bill Wallace was a smart-ass. But then, who was going to do anything about it? One day only Bill and I were in the studio. He told me to bend my knees all the way with my hands clasped behind my head and leap as high into the air as I could while moving around the room. As I was doing this, he went into his office, put his feet on his desk, and read the newspaper. When he was finished he came back into the large room and said, "What the hell are you doing that for? You look like a damn bunny rabbit." Bill was beyond excellent; he was the best. He could kick you three times in the head before you could block. What an athlete! His school was the "Harvard" of Tae Kwon Do schools. It was later purchased by Herb Johnson, ranked 5th in the U.S. in full contact TKO. Bob Berry and I were lucky to live in Indianapolis and have this school readily available.

After Elvis Presley died, Bill Wallace became Dan Akroyd's and John Belushi's bodyguard. I guess you all know what happened to John Belushi. You can hire someone to protect the outside; you can't hire someone to protect the inside. As an adoptee, this is especially significant. For adoptees, many times there is a feeling of isolation, a feeling that there is no one around who can understand what you have gone through: the war, the orphanage, the adoption and integration-into-a-different-culture process. You are left to wade through society by yourself and deal with the various prejudices that arise. At these times, you have to be *extra* careful not to use alcohol or drugs because you are more than normally drawn to the temporary relief these substances will bring. I am grateful for my Tae Kwon Do training because respect for tradition, for one's instructor and one's own body are an integral part of the program.

University Life

After attending IUPUI for a year, I went to Indiana University in Bloomington, Indiana, to pursue an undergraduate degree in psychology. I lived there in a close community called the Living Learning Center near the Health, Physical Education and Recreation (HPER) building and tennis courts. This was my first experience living in a dorm. My new roommate didn't know quite what to make of me. One day I was practicing with homemade nun-chucks as Steve, my roommate, sat studying at his desk. Nun-chucks are a defensive device used in Tae Kwon Do consisting of two stout sticks held together by a chain. While I was using the nun-chucks that day it broke and one stick flew through the glass of our window. Steve stood up, closed his book, walked out of the room and I never saw him again. For the rest of the year I had a double dorm room to myself. It was great!

I was once arrested by New York State troopers for having a pair of nun-chucks in plain view in my car. They handcuffed me. My brother Richard and my sister Leslie had to follow behind the trooper car to their post where I had mug shots and fingerprints taken. As we were waiting for the judge to wake up at 3:00 a.m. to take care of the situation, the troopers wanted me to give them a nun-chuck demonstration. I did not. It was an odd request.

The judge finally appeared looking bleary-eyed and wearing his slippers, looked at the arresting officers and said, "Don't you know nun-chucks aren't against the law until next October?" We had to negotiate a fine anyway. We negotiated because we needed gasoline money to complete the drive to Indiana. As in all walks of life, there are good troopers and bad troopers. I hope the good troopers outnumber the bad.

The kids across the hall from me in the dormitory were partying types. They were like the "Three Stooges," Jeff, Bill and Eric. I had a habit of renaming people to better fit their personality. Eric was very spastic in personality, talking about this and that. I renamed him "Erratic." Everyone called him Erratic after that because it definitely fit him. Another guy who lived down the hall was Joe Haleman, a Vietnam veteran, most proud of his scrapbook of photos showing dead Vietnamese, displaying them as though they were trophy animals in some great game hunt. I hated those photos. I renamed him "GI Joe." When GI Joe first met me, he didn't like me because I looked Asian. One day while I was sitting in my room studying, he walked up to me and put a .44 magnum gun to my temple and said, "What are you going to do now, big guy?"

I answered, "I'm going to kill you." I guess he liked that answer because it was macho enough for him so he pointed the barrel up in the air and eased the hammer back down. He was a real bully. His attitude didn't change toward me until one day, as I was studying in my room, the door opened and a small entourage of people came in, perhaps eight or nine along with GI Joe. Scott, a fellow student, said, "GI Joe doesn't believe that you can break a board with just your big toe. Show him, Tom!"

I said, "You're right Joe, I can't break a board with my big toe, but I can break two." I got two boards and had two students hold them securely about four feet from the floor. I broke both using just my big toe as point of contact. GI Joe was impressed. He respected me a lot after that. He wanted me to teach him Tae Kwon Do. I told him he should join our class and that I taught over 100 students Friday evenings.

GI Joe was a dedicated Tae Kwon Do student; he didn't miss a class. However, after he attended several classes, a friend of mine came to me looking somewhat beat-up. In tears he said, "I was in a stall in the men's room and Joe kicked the door in and started kicking and beating up on me for no reason." The next day we had Tae Kwon Do class. Joe came in. The class had all heard what he had done. I walked up to him, grabbed him by his collar and slammed him up against the wall, lifting him up off the ground a couple of inches. I yelled in his face, "Don't you ever use Tae Kwon Do to hurt anyone ever again. You're out of here. Don't ever come back!" I am not normally a violent person. However, Tae Kwon Do is very important to me. It is not intended to be about violence. Just the opposite, it is intended to tame the spirit while strengthening the body. What GI Joe had done was outrageous in my mind.

Later, I was driving down a one-way street behind my dormitory when Joe, driving a white van, stopped in the middle of the road and jumped out with a rifle encased in a leather holder. He was trying to get the rifle free of the case but the scope had caught on the zipper. I floored my car and drove right up to him; I slammed on my brakes, turning my car sideways so as to miss him. He looked at me sheepishly. He knew I could have hurt or killed him. He smiled and said, "I owe you one," got back in his van and drove away. No one ever saw Joe after that; he left school. Who knows what he's doing now? Actually, Joe was a good guy. The Vietnam War had messed up his mind as it did for many people. I know. It takes a strong personality to go through that kind of experience unaffected. I wish I could have helped Joe. I hope GI Joe finds inner peace, if he's still among us.

One Saturday my friend James and I went to Nashville, Tennessee, to a karate tournament because he wanted to see me fight. I usually fought in the middleweight division. It was a rule that whatever weight class you fought in, you could also fight in any weight class above your classification. I decided to fight in the heavyweight division. Although those guys were huge and very powerful, they were a bit slower. Everyone who fights knows that speed is everything. I bowed into the first fight. My opponent was a "brother" who was perhaps 6' 5", weighing in at around 250 lbs. I was 6' 1" and about 175 lbs. It was a strange, short fight. We bowed in; I jumped across the gap and kicked him in the side of the head. He went down like a pile of bricks. The refs all stood up and a doctor came forward. The fight was over.

In the crowd of people after the fight, the guy I knocked down located me and tapped me on the shoulder. He asked, "Are you mad at me?"

I said, "Excuse me?"

He asked, "Did I offend you in any way before the fight?"

I answered, "No brother. I don't even know you. I don't dislike you."

"It seemed like you hated me or something, like you had something against me. I didn't even see the kick coming," he said.

I answered, "I noticed."

He asked, "How did you do that?"

How I got my kicks in college

I thought for a while. What could I tell this guy? I said, "After we bowed in, you were out of focus; your consciousness was somewhere else, maybe was out in the crowd. I think maybe you were concerned about how good you were going to look to your girlfriend or your friends. I think about only one thing when I am going into a match and maybe you should too. I think TKO-ASAP. It's not like we're in there dancing or anything. You're trying to knock me out and I'm trying to knock you out. Focus on one simple little thing, TKO-ASAP." We clasped hands together in friendship and he walked away shaking his head. This was the first and only tournament my friend James had ever seen. He thought I always fought like that.

I didn't always do as well in the fights but I have never been knocked out. The Tae Kwon Do Federation continually changed the rules in fighting, which was difficult for me. I was one of four corner judges in the last tournament I attended. After that I just concentrated on teaching. My students would come in first, second and third. I trained them on an electronic reaction timer. If you can get your punch or kick below the magic 27 millisecond time barrier, you can hit your opponent without them being physically able to react. Twenty-seven milliseconds was the magic number.

Tae Kwon Do is for defense, but sometimes the best defense is a hellacious offense. However, it is always better to talk your way out of a fight rather than ruin someone's ego so that they have no choice but to come at you with a gun at a later point in time. Don't you think so?

Hobie Billingsley was the diving coach at IU. I took diving class with him to learn to handle myself in the air. The class started first thing in the morning which is the nightmare of any college student: to wake up and dive into freezing water morning after morning. There were at least 30 of us in this class. We learned many dives on the lower diving board. After we perfected the dives to the best of our ability on this lower board, we progressed to the higher board.

For any of you who have made this transition, you know what a difference in timing and water impact there is! The very first morning when we tried out the higher board, this reality hit all of us, literally. From the ground the upper board really doesn't look very frightening, but when you go up there, it is. Upon my first attempt I under-rotated and smacked my groin upon entry. Did that smart! It felt just like the time I got kicked in the groin in a karate tournament. I slowly swam to the side of the pool where Hobie stood. After catching my breath I got out of the water and stood in line for another attempt.

As everyone tried this new distance and came out of the pool with about the same impression, a funny thing started to happen. Every time I got out of the water to stand in line, the line wasn't moving. Everyone was afraid to go. So I worked my way up to the front of the line and tried it again and again until I started not hurting myself. I tried a flip; I tried a backflip.

I walked up the ladder and was just about to take my steps when the coach called, "Tom, wait right there!" He addressed the rest of the class. He said, "You see that guy up there? He has experienced everything all of you have experienced this morning. This is a sport where you find out about yourself. This is more than just diving; this is about character! Look at him. Most of you don't want to go off the higher board anymore and won't go up there to give it another try. He keeps cutting in line and going at it! Go ahead, Tom."

Was I ever embarrassed. There I was in my little skimpies with

Cliff Diving at Agawa Bay, Canada

everyone staring at me. Thanks a lot, Hobie! I just figured, "Hey, I'm already awake this morning, why not? The more I do this painful thing, the less painful it gets." I love physical sports. If it requires movement, I'm there! Years later, Hobie was picked to be an Olympic diving coach. He was exceptional.

I have to confess something: After my heroics that day on the high dive, my testicles swelled to the size of oranges. I had to be admitted to the University Health Center for several days. I hurt like hell and had to suffer the indignity of being inspected several times a day. I didn't mind the doctors looking but I noticed that a half dozen or more nurses and nurses' aides managed to be in the vicinity of my "unveilings." I must have looked like the prize boar at the state fair.

After I recovered I spent a few days cutting class with my buddies, diving at the quarries where the movie *Breaking Away* was filmed. Some students were injured there due to the height of the cliffs. They'd land wrong or hit the limestone rocks below. It was a restricted area because of this but we would sneak in anyway. It still is a beautiful secluded place for diving and swimming if you don't get arrested.

Carpentry

After graduating from Indiana University with a bachelor's degree in psychology, I encountered a difficulty that my father had foreseen: there isn't much you can do in the U.S. with an undergraduate degree in psychology, directly in the field of psychology, that is. To practice as a clinical psychologist it takes at least a master's degree and preferably a Ph.D. For me to have pursued an advanced degree in psychology would have put me in competition with· many students who had had better early schooling than I did, particularly in language skills.

Instead of continuing my college education I moved to Brown County, Indiana, and obtained employment with a construction crew building houses. In three months I became the supervisor. My attitude toward manual labor was that the harder and faster you worked, the better. I felt that hard work was physically good for you. I still do.

Gary was the owner of the business. One day we decided we needed to hire another employee, someone with a lot of carpentry experience. The following week Gary told me that after interviewing some applicants he picked Dan, because Dan said he had been a carpenter all his life. The first day on the job Dan showed up with a new tool belt, a hammer, and a tape measure. These were all the tools of the trade he owned. It was soon apparent that this new employee knew little or nothing of the trade. I said to him, "Dan, I thought you were experienced and knew everything about carpentry."

He answered, "I've been a carpenter all my life. My name is Dan Carpenter." Yes indeed, his name was really Dan Carpenter and this was his first job ever in the building trade. It turned out that Dan was a quick study with all the energy and great sense of humor one could hope for. We became the best of friends, building many houses together. My experience from that job was invaluable. Today, when I need the flooring replaced in the bathroom, new walls, electrical, plumbing, I do it myself.

Stepping backward in time for a moment, I remember talking to a Nigerian doctor at a party in my parents' home while I was in high school. The doctor said to me and others having a conversation with him, "America has a secret weapon you are not even aware of…the secret is your respect for people who do manual things well. I grew up in a nation influenced by the English disdain for manual workers. I was taught that it was preferable to do anything, even nothing, rather than be identified as a 'worker.' I had lived in America as an undergraduate student for a number of years before I learned of America's almost unique respect for craftsmanship, even the ability to dig a good straight ditch. I worked for a Detroit athletic club that catered to high-level automotive company executives, picking up towels and doing other janitorial chores. After several months of this I heard enough locker room conversations among the club members to realize that they had done things similar to what I was doing while in school and viewed it as perfectly normal. I said to myself at the time, 'These Americans are fantastic. They have erased boundaries that exist in almost every other culture.' I still feel that way…and that is America's secret weapon."

Back to the carpentry business: Dan and I were finishing up a garage job which had an adjoining wooden fence. The garage was located very far away from town, hence far from the store where we bought the stain for the fence. I was applying the stain to the fencing at the bottom of a little hill some distance from where Dan was cutting off the tops of the fence posts with a handsaw. As I painted, my mind ran through a gambit of thoughts. During these thoughts, I saw a full paint can suddenly spill over, spraying the contents into the air. I went back to other thoughts. Five minutes later Dan applied his last stroke to the fence post top, and as the piece of wood came free from the rest of the post, he accidentally punched the piece with his fist, the fist grasping the handsaw. The wood slid straight down the saw blade, down the hill and hit my paint can squarely, spraying the contents everywhere. It was exactly as I had seen it five minutes before in my thoughts. We had to drive quite a long distance and purchase another can of stain to finish the job.

When Dan and I constructed the future home of our friend, Gary Deever, a lot of trees and brush were cleared and burned in an open field. A few days later a bulldozer operator filled the back of a wooden flatbed truck with the debris from the burning for a trip to the landfill, with me driving the truck. The road I took between Columbus, Indiana, and Nashville is long and straight. As I drove, my mind turned to an unfortunate accident involving a gasoline tank truck that had occurred a short time before in Florida. In that accident people at a nearby beach had been sprayed with flaming gasoline. I thought of the gasoline tank on the flatbed truck and visualized myself having to choose between flaming gasoline and driving myself intentionally into a ditch to escape the flames. While my mind was occupied with these thoughts I glanced into the rearview mirror of my truck and was astounded to see the whole back of the truck had 12- to-15 foot flames billowing high and far behind it.

I jammed on the brakes and jumped out of the truck. The burning brush pile apparently had hot ashes hidden deep inside and the wind from driving down the road fanned them into a huge blaze. There was a long line of vehicles trailing far behind me, because burning debris had been flying out the back of the truck. As luck would have it the very first vehicle behind me was a pickup truck driven by a Fish & Game Department person carrying 55-gallon drums of water and fish. Other vehicles pulled up to help. We made a bucket brigade and extinguished the fire. The back of the wooden truck was badly burned, but the gas tank had not caught on fire. We were very fortunate. Gary and Dave thought it was funny. I didn't care because it wasn't my truck and no one got hurt.

On our time off Dan and I did some fun things. He lived on a farm where, in return for low rent, he took care of the animals. We decided to ride a bull that was standing in an open pasture. After flipping a coin to see who had to go first, we walked cautiously out into the open field and up to the bull. Dan lost the toss so it was his turn first. He is quite a bit shorter than I. Dan stood next to the bull and thought he could swing his right leg up and over it in one motion, like they do in the cowboy movies. Because he is not as tall as a cowboy, when he kicked his foot out and swung his leg over, he accidentally kicked the bull right in its rear end before landing squarely on the bull's back.

It may have been a combination of being kicked in the rear and having someone jump on his back all in one motion that caused the bull to buck Dan off immediately. After Dan landed on the ground next to me, the bull did exactly what you see in the movies. He lowered his head and stamped his hooves into the ground before charging. Dan and I ran for our lives and hid behind a little cluster of trees until we had the chance to run across the open field and jump over the fence. He then tried to talk me into taking my turn at it because he had just taken his turn. I said, "I'm not going to ride the bull after you kicked it in his butt! That wasn't in the deal!" We still laugh about that day.

On a different construction crew, we had to dig a footer on each side of a house so we could build walls up and over the existing dwelling. There were four of us to dig the footer. The foreman said to us, "OK you guys, you three start digging the footer on this side. Tom, you come with me and dig the footer on the other side. When you get finished come over here and help these guys out." We all laughed. The foreman left.

I went to the other side where a string line marked where the footer should go. I started digging like a maniac. I love digging. When I tired from digging with the shovel in one position, I shifted the shovel to the other side and dug with my other hand holding the shovel as the lead hand. It's a trick I learned when young. If you always hold the shovel in one way you tire half of your body. If you reverse your hands you use totally different muscles which have not been working hard at all. Every person is, in a sense, really two people. Humans are bilateral with two arms and two legs connected together down the middle. Even our cerebral cortex has two different hemispheres connected together by our corpus callosum. The two hemispheres are different. Each hemisphere majors in specific information processing. While you sleep the information in the two hemispheres continues to integrate.

After I finished the footer on my side of the house, I walked over to the other side where the other three were working. They were only half done. One had stopped working altogether and sat smoking a cigarette. The other two were digging very slowly. They were not pleased about digging a footer when they were carpenters. I told them, "The sooner we get this done, the sooner we can get on to the fun stuff." I went to work with them and when the foreman came back to the site, we only had six or seven feet to go. He walked to my original side of the house and came back to where we were working with a grin on his face. He knew what had happened and he liked my attitude.

Family Matters

While I was working at carpentry I got married to Licia, whom I had known at Indiana University. Licia and I had dated for a while and when we graduated from Indiana University and found jobs, it seemed natural for us to marry and raise a family. We bought a house in the midst of the Yellowwood Forest. Our first house wasn't fancy. It had a rough-sawn exterior and interior with a centrally located wood-burning stove for a source of heat in the four rooms. It got a bit chilly in the back bedroom on winter nights.

We later had twin girls. When I called my father from the hospital and told him of the birth of the twins, he replied, "That's odd...there aren't any twins on our side of the family. It must be from her side of the family."

I said, "Dad...I'm adopted...remember?" We had a good laugh. While my beautiful children were growing up I was a very patient father. Rather than having knee-jerk reactions to various things they did, I tried to understand the reasons why so I could react more appropriately.

One day I was putting up drywall in the twins' bedroom. The day before, I had completed the room right next to their bedroom. It was all painted and trimmed out. While I was placing new drywall in their bedroom I kept hearing a faint "rap-a-tap-tap" sound. For a long time I didn't think much of it. I finally stuck my head out their bedroom door to see about the continuing noise. There, right on the other side of the wall I was working on, Jennifer and Jessica were standing side by side, meticulously hammering a row of drywall nails into the finished painted wall. They were only four years old at the time. Halfway around the room was a row of perhaps over a hundred drywall nails, all next to each other at their eye level. The normal parental response might have been to hit them, or yell or punish. I thought, "How cute, they're mimicking me!" They were hard at work and it was excellent hand-eye coordination for them. It was also good experience for them to learn how to use a hammer without hitting their fingers. They did an excellent job. I was proud of them.

Jessica and Jennifer (wading waifs)

Another time we found an oak captain's chair which needed to be stripped of its old paint and restained. Jennifer was very young, but she'd watched me work on furniture for hours. She watched as I took stain and a cloth and restained the chair. It had a lot of pieces and many nooks and crannies. After it dried we brought it upstairs into the bedroom. One day while sitting for the kids, I noticed that Jessica was playing downstairs while Jennifer had gone upstairs. Jennifer was very quiet for quite a long time, too long. I went up to make sure she was okay. She was on her last little spindle. She had taken Vaseline Intensive Care and a cloth and had covered absolutely every inch of surface of this very ornately carved chair! What a sweetheart. She had done a splendid job. She did not miss a spot. I picked her up and gave her a big hug and kiss and said "Oh sweetheart, how wonderful! Let's go downstairs now and see what else we can do." After I got her involved in other things, I ran upstairs with some spray cleaner and a roll of paper towels and quickly as possible removed all the Vaseline. What a hard-working little girl. Perhaps when she grows older she will be in the furniture business. Parents, don't hit your children. Try to understand their actions. They are doing something they have seen you or someone else do.

One morning I awakened to screaming from downstairs. Licia, Jennifer, and Jessica came running up the stairs screaming that there was a blacksnake in the bathroom. I walked downstairs and sure enough, there was a six-foot blacksnake staring at me in the bathroom. It turned and started slithering behind the space between the sink cabinet and the wall. I grabbed the snake by the tail and began to tug. It was extremely difficult to pull it out. When its head came clear of the cabinet it turned and tried to bite me, so I let go. It once again started to slither behind the cabinet.

I yelled, "Get me a pillowcase!" I grabbed the tail harder and again began to pull. This time when it tried to bite me, I held up the open pillowcase and it lunged into the open sack. I shook the rest of the snake into the pillowcase and tied the opening. Instead of letting the snake loose outside where it might find its way back into the house, I decided to take it for a ride down to a farm and release it.

While I was driving the pickup truck down dirt roads, the snake was standing up in the closed pillowcase. I drove faster. As I approached a bend in the road, I looked over at the pillowcase once more. It was completely flat; the snake was on the loose in my truck. I jammed on the brakes in the middle of the road, opened the truck door and fell out onto the road on my back. After a few minutes the snake slithered out of the truck and into the field. I was happy to see him go.

Actually, blacksnakes are very good for the environment. They eat mice and rats and anything else they can catch. Although they can grow very large, they are not poisonous. This was not the smallest one in our neck of the woods. One day we saw a snake long enough to extend all the way from one side of the road to the other. We thought it was a fallen tree branch until it started to slither away. Blacksnakes are extremely fast and it hurts when they bite. The best thing to do is leave them alone and go about your business.

Through my wife's family I became friends with Nichol Williamson, the stage and movie actor. Nichol was married for a time to my wife's sister. I liked Nichol because he stuck up for me when no one else would. He did not like to go to social affairs, so he gave me his invitation to the premiere of *The Pirates of Penzance*. I had never been to a private party with so many celebrities. He lent me a black velvet tux and I accompanied his wife. At the party, I saw Christopher Reeve prior to his terrible horse accident.

There were many movie directors and other celebrities like Morgan Fairchild. We danced on a dance floor which was filled knee high with fog from dry ice. It was amazing. Thank you, Nichol. I put my fist into the air and crank up that Scottish music to you! What a wild man! Approach at your own risk! He helped me more than once. He bought me a microscope in New York City which I still have. What a rowdy guy. We went hiking and camping in the mountains of Montana with an interesting group of people. Ah, those were the days. No matter where we went everyone recognized him. People who were wannabe actors were too intimidated to speak to him; they would melt or fall apart. But I was not in the entertainment business; we treated each other as regular people.

In New York City where Nichol lived at the time, we once attended the "Saturday Night Live" show. Nichol was given free tickets. We got to go to the head of the waiting line and were standing around the door in front of the studio when Howard Cosell, recognizing Nichol, came walking over and shook Nichol's hand. Howard said, in his gravelly Cosell voice, "Good evening Nichol! How have you been doing?"

Nichol put on a fake grin and answered, "Oh just fine, just fine." As Howard turned to go up on stage, because he was in the show, Nichol leaned over to my ear and asked, "Who the heck was that?"

I said, "Nichol! That was Howard Cosell. You know! *Howard Cosell*!" Nichol is such a kidder. To this day I don't know if he recognized Howard.

Human Services

After a couple of years I grew tired of building houses. It didn't matter what the weather was, my good-natured crew and I would gamely build houses; in the record blizzard of 1978, in rain or 100 degree temperatures, we worked. I decided that an indoor job might be a little better than outdoor employment. After looking around, I gained employment with a federal government-funded community effort that provided weatherization in low-income housing. It was a worthy cause. Some people in the U.S. cannot afford to repair their homes and make them airtight so they'll stay warm during the winter months. We assessed the income of these people, and if they were eligible for assistance according to federal guidelines, we insulated their homes, storm windows and doors; repaired floors and cracks; and replaced windows at no cost to the homeowner. It was a multi-layered mission. The individuals who did the work were a varied lot. Some had no carpentry experience and needed employment and training, some had carpentry experience and simply needed a job. Some of the employees were ex-convicts and needed a fresh start. Before I left the program I supervised 87 people. My experiences in that period could fill their own book. Some examples:

I had to carry a beeper because we covered a large geographic area. I got a call from one of the crews saying I had to get to another county ASAP. I jumped into my truck and sped to their job site, where I was told that one of my employees was blown away on drugs and wasn't moving. I could see from the truck who it was. I walked up to him and said, "Hey Jimmy! What's going on?" He was frozen to the corner of a trailer, holding a level so that it appeared as though he was working, leveling the trailer. But he wasn't moving; he was frozen. I got a little closer and yelled much more loudly, "Hey Jimmy!! What's going on!" Still no answer and still no movement. I finally got right in his ear and yelled, "JIMMY!!!"

Slowly, as though he were a poorly oiled droid, he turned his head and with the rest of his body frozen, answered in the tiniest little voice, "What?" (By the way, this guy was 6'3" and after years of being in the pen, was pumped up to look like a weightlifter).

I asked him again, "What's going on?"

He answered in the same tiny voice, "I'm working." I told him I wanted to see him next to my truck. He slowly let go of the level, stood up and walked behind me over to the truck. I informed him that this was the last time he was going to come to work under the influence and drove away. I was told that after I left he went up to another employee who had also done time and asked, "Who snitched on me? You snitched on me, didn't you?"

Ben answered, "Don't mess with me man, I'll just kill you."

Jimmy turned to a third employee and asked, "Did you snitch on me?"

This person picked up a 2x4 and said, "Yea, what are you going to do about it?" Needless to say, this prompted a fight. I was paged again to return to the job site.

I told Jimmy to leave the job site immediately. After he left, I got in my truck and went back to the office, but Jimmy returned to the site and continued to harass the employees, so the local police were called. Jimmy came into my office. He wanted to fight. I told him, "Don't mess with me, Jimmy, I'll take your head off." He left and I never saw him after that. I heard he was later arrested for rape and armed robbery. He's back lifting weights.

The following morning I was in my office and two employees burst into the door with frightened looks on their faces. I heard loud yelling coming from the main office so I walked out to assess the commotion. A female employee was holding a gun to her husband's stomach, also a co-worker. I asked her to give me the gun. She refused. I then told her husband to please leave the office immediately. He left and got into his truck. I went back to my office. She then went out to the main street and emptied the gun at the fleeing truck. Because of this she was promptly terminated. She hired a lawyer to file a sex discrimination suit which was later dropped.

At Christmas the company had a party for all its employees, their friends, and spouses. At the party a really obnoxious guy, Travis, was moving from group to group making a nuisance of himself by saying improper things to wives and girlfriends. Sylvester

Tutt, the executive director, was pretty fed up with this guy but did not know what to do.

Around two in the morning as the party wound down, a large group of us were standing in the middle of the gym floor making small talk before going home. I was dressed in a suit and tie because I was an administrator. Many of the employees from my department were there. For no reason, perhaps because I was dressed in a suit and tie, the obnoxious guy, Travis, pointed to me and announced "I bet I could kick his butt!"

The second he said this, Sylvester kicked off his shoe, pulled out a crisp hundred dollar bill, slammed it on the table, pointed to me and said, "I'll bet one hundred dollars on Tom."

Everyone was shocked and silent. A lot of my fellow workers respected me very much. Many of them were ex-cons and were very experienced at street fighting. But they had total respect for me because they knew I was a tournament fighter and a Tae Kwon Do instructor. I was on the spot. I couldn't back down or talk myself out of this one because I would lose respect and credibility with the people who worked in my department. Travis had a bad reputation for beating women and threatening people at knife point. I said to Travis, "Hey man, you really don't want to do this. Let's be friends."

Travis boasted, "Ah, you're nothin' but a chicken shit. I'm gonna kick your ass."

I said again, "You really don't want to do this!" Looking around, I could see that all the employees were standing in a huge circle. There was no way to bow out and still have respect.

I walked over to a chair and took off my tie, shoes, socks and shirt. This threw Travis off balance right away. Actually, he looked pretty worried. I got back into the circle, stood in the center and got down in my normal tournament stance with my feet spread apart, standing sideways to Travis. Travis still had on his black leather jacket and looked rough, tough, and very worried.

Without going into any details, I can say it only took a second for him to drop to the floor. He wouldn't get up...refused to get up. I went back to the chair, got dressed and left. The next day the executive director came to my office, smiling ear to ear, and apologized for putting me on the spot. He promised he would never do that again. He had just gotten sick and tired of Travis.

At this point of my life I was probably at the peak of my physical strength. Although I didn't go looking for trouble, I had reached a stage where inwardly I felt I was no longer a vulnerable *tuki*.

Moving Toward Technology

In 1983, five years after receiving a degree in psychology from Indiana University, I assessed my chances of ever being satisfied doing the kind of work that was available to me with my education to date. I discussed my situation with my father and his wife, Suzanne, and they suggested that I obtain a scholarship to continue my college education, this time in *engineering*. I looked blankly at them without comprehension. Scholarship! How, where? God bless them, they had apparently noted my increasing dissatisfaction with my lack of career opportunities and had decided even before I approached them, that they would pay my tuition to engineering college when I was ready. *Was I ever ready!*

There was a condition attached to their offer. They practiced the philosophy, "We help those who help themselves." As a matter of fact my brother, sisters and I were brought up with this concept. We children always worked for things, even when it wasn't strictly necessary, so as to appreciate the value of money. When my father and Suzanne made the offer to help me return to college, I readily agreed to continue to work while pursuing an engineering degree.

I returned to school at IUPUI in Indianapolis and received a bachelor's degree in electronic engineering from Purdue University after four years of work and study. While in school I worked for Wavetec Corporation, which was also located in Indianapolis. Since Licia worked in Bloomington, we continued to live in Bloomington and I commuted 50 miles each way to Indianapolis every day. I also attended engineering classes three evenings a week and had a heavy load of homework to do besides. This made for a long day. Four or five hours of sleep per night was my average rest. Again I had reason to thank God and my birth parents for a strong constitution. And, I had my adoptive father and his warm and caring wife to thank for believing in me and providing love, guidance and financial support.

I started at Wavetec as a troubleshooting technician on the factory floor. There were 1,400 employees at the plant when I started. Soon after, during some hard economic times, the company had to

Richard Clement, Sr. and Suzanne

lay off 400 workers. I then was transferred to the Component Manufacturing Department. There the Attenuator Department had a
mini-crisis on their hands. The Engineering Department had engineered a DC Microwave Attenuator used in communication equipment and the production department had manufactured quite a few
of them, hundreds of thousands of dollars worth. However, none of
them could be shipped due to a multitude of problems. I was moved
to this department in a last-ditch effort to save the project. After observing a couple hundred of these devices under a microscope, it was
apparent to me that each one of them had undergone numerous repairs, some of which caused even greater damage. I introduced the
practice of serializing each attenuator, making it possible to create a
written history of repairs for each specific unit. For the first time the
department was able to complete and ship the attenuators to its customers. I had *personal experience* of having no history files. It is
hard to fix a problem without history.

While in this department I came up with an invention—a surface
mounted, flat disc, rotary microwave attenuator. Some name, huh?
The difference between this invention and the old model was that the
previous one had to be manually assembled and tuned, whereas the
new ones could simply be assembled by a programmed robotic arm
and placed on a conveyor belt for mass infra-red soldering. My
supervisor praised me saying, "Most people only come up with one
invention in all their lives. This is yours. Congratulations." Two
months later I came up with my second invention. He seemed taken
aback and said that I was now part of a more elite group of inventors
with two inventions. After a period of time, I produced a third. This
greatly increased my confidence that engineering was definitely the
field where I was most suited.

After working in the microwave attenuator department for a
couple of months, I wanted to try out a new idea, a small round circuit board which could drastically save both manufacturing time and
cost. A "time line" is a method whereby a project is organized by
listing every step that needs to be taken from the beginning to com-
pletion and a time interval assigned to each element. I was very excited to see if there was any merit in the new circuit board I had in
mind. I brought a rough drawing to the head of the drafting depart-

ment and explained the details of the design. This person, Steve, thought it was a good idea and informed me that his department was backed up for at least two to three months. My heart sank. I didn't want to wait that long for a drawing of the circuit. This was only one of many steps needed to have a finished prototype in my hand to test. I thought to myself, "How in the world does anything get done around here? It's going to take over half a year to get a proto circuit."

I went back to my desk and pulled out all my drafting tools from school and began to design the board. The drawing was ten times scale and required reduction in the photo lab to actual size. I completed the drawing the next day. The time line had been condensed by two to three months. I brought the draft to the photo lab. There was usually a three-week backlog in the lab due to many projects being submitted by many engineers. This would not do! A lady named Beth was working in the lab on this particular day. We were not close friends but would always say "hello" in the hallways. She told me, "If you can wait ten minutes until my break time, I'll photo your circuit then." What a relief! I sat and talked and laughed about anything and everything while she did her job and handed me the negatives and a print in what seemed like no time.

I carried the photos to the circuit board etching fabrication department. This was a large department with many employees and lots of dangerous chemicals and odors. To my relief two acquaintances, Danny and Bill, worked in this area and met me at the door. Bill took the print from my hand, winked, and said, "Will tomorrow be okay?" Tomorrow??? That was absolutely phenomenal!

The next day as promised, I had 64 circuit boards on my desk ready to test. It was an exciting time for me. I soldered components to the boards and sat at my lab bench *tweaking* this and that to improve the performance of the new design. A senior engineer walking by suddenly stopped. He removed his glasses and looked all over my table at the circuits and test equipment, back at me again, and said, "What the hell is this?"

I answered, "A proto of the new circuit we were talking about earlier this week." I thought he was going to go into cardiac arrest. What normally takes half a year took less than a week. I called it "time compression." A tech complained to the "higher ups" about my non-compliance with procedure. He was immediately squelched.

I was next promoted to a new position, Supervisor of Engineering/Production, with the responsibility for integrating the efforts of the two departments. Prior to this, these departments were not communicating efficiently to produce a final product which could be shipped. Sometimes when I tracked down the engineer who designed the circuit boards and brought him onto the floor to help with troubleshooting, he would say, "I had no idea this design would work, let alone have it released to the floor." We saw; we fixed; we conquered.

Wavetec had a think tank. Senior electrical engineers would get together in the conference room to brainstorm and problem-solve. After one meeting, a senior engineer caught up with me in the hallway and said, "I don't know how you do it. It's like we are all in there bumping into each other in the dark and you came in and flipped on the light switch." It was the nicest compliment anyone could ever hope to receive. It made me forget the long hours I was spending commuting to work, going to college at night and arriving home tired and hungry after 11 p.m.

For an outlet from work and study I joined a company soccer team. Various employees wanted to form a team. We had a meeting with all interested parties and it became apparent that I was the only one with previous soccer experience. The others, although very athletic and highly motivated, only had experience in American sports such as basketball, football and baseball. We made out a practice schedule whereby we would meet at a local field to train. I found that not only were the other players all lacking in soccer skills, they had no clue as to the rules of the game.

We had to start with the basics. Many of them could not kick the ball. After the first practice I went home to create a plan of attack. The next practice was a lesson in Tae Kwon Do warm-up exercises followed by simply *how to kick the damn ball*. Quite a few of them made the classic mistake when trying to kick the ball. They would start kicking before lifting their knee. When kicking in this manner whip-lash occurs to the knee. The correct Tae Kwon Do method of kicking is to first lift the knee and then kick, thus avoiding whiplash. Standard drills were practiced over and over and over again. The team next signed up for the International Soccer League in Indianapolis as the newest member.

I thought we were well prepared for our debut before the public, but when the game began, everything I had drilled into them about playing positions went out the window and all ten players, minus the goalie, jumped on the ball, kicking wildly and at random. Our hard work and dedication, practicing three times per week for months through rain, sleet, and snow, finally paid off with our losing by a score of 27-0. Our team was unable to get the darned ball past their goalie. Back to the drawing board! We decided to practice every other day and on weekends. We practiced and practiced and practiced. A sense of teamwork developed and we began functioning as a group, not as a bunch of individual jocks.

This soccer league was comprised of many teams from many different nationalities: British, Spanish, Irish, Italian, and German and we were known as the "Crazy American Team." We were the worst. After weeks of diligent practice, our next game approached with the Italian team as our opponent. The final score ended with us losing 24-1. I'm still not sure how our one ball got by their goalie. After working on our skills again we played the Vietnamese team. The score was 17-2. We made two goals because their goalie was not in the box. He had grown bored of being alone at their end of the field and was up with the rest of the team making goals against us.

After every game we improved and we kept practicing. Eventually, after a period of two years, we began to win. After two and a half years we became the second in the league and were awarded not only the Most Improved Team award but the Most Difficult to Beat. Sometimes we won by a score of 7-1; other times it was 2-0. We continued with our winning ways until I left the company and found employment elsewhere.

After working at Wavetec for three years I got an offer to work in the Research and Development Department at Vantec Inc., a urological medical device company located close to my home in Bloomington. Vantec Inc. was a spin-off of Cook Urological Company located in Spencer, Indiana. The production department of Vantec was located in an old building once occupied by a car sales com-

The Crazy American Team

pany. In order to get to the Research and Development Department, you had to enter the production plant, traverse the plant to the far side, pass into a separate room which was used as a Quality Control Department, and enter the bathroom. Once in the bathroom you had to open a closet door and walk into the closet. The doorway at the back of the closet opened into the R&D room where I worked. I have described the circuitous route we took to get to the place we worked in order to emphasize the manner in which many small start-up firms operate during their early years. New, small companies start with an idea, courage and some cash. Luckily, America has an abundance of all three.

The room I worked in had no windows. The R&D manager,

Carolyn, and I were the only ones in the department. We worked on a number of devices there. Once in a while a urologist would visit and talk to us about various devices.

It was in the R&D room that I invented my first medical device. Prior to my invention, "pumping syringes" worked with a spring to refill the syringe after the syringe contents were discharged. My invention, which was patented by Vantec, relied on self-generated vacuum to refill the syringe, thus eliminating the spring and several plastic parts. Many doctors have operated the syringe and looked at me with a smile saying, "There's a spring in this, right?" No, there was no spring. The vacuum acted as the spring. They would then reply, "It's like magic!"

It wasn't magic. It was an inventive way to reduce the cost and bulk of a syringe in large demand in the medical field. There have probably been over a million of these funny syringes sold to the medical field by now. They are used, for example, in manual irrigation systems to transfer fluid from a saline bag to an operative site.

Encouraged by my first success in medical product design, I started working on more and more projects. At one time I was working on over 50 different products. Attending operations and observing surgeons do the best they could with the instruments available was the most important education anyone could ever get in the field of device development. I began to observe more and more operations, visiting the Mayo Clinic in Minnesota, Baylor School of Medicine, Yale School of Medicine, Methodist Hospital in Indianapolis, and Stanford School of Medicine, to name only a few.

It was because of the need to improve so many products that I went from an engineer to an imagineer. There is a world of difference between an engineer and an imagineer. An engineer has the correct schooling and theories floating around his head to solve technical problems and come up with nifty solutions. Usually, many of the engineers I've talked to tell me that after work they leave their job behind. This is where the worlds drift apart. Here is an exercise that an imagineer must master. Imagineers can work on problem-solving no matter where they are, driving to and from work, waiting in a grocery line, eating lunch or dinner, swimming in a lake, whatever.

To do this successfully requires exercise. This is the exercise:

first practice with your eyes closed, then you should be able to do this exercise with your eyes wide open. (It is so much easier to drive a car with your eyes open.) Close your eyes and imagine a small Ping-Pong ball floating about a foot above your head. It is white. See that it is white. Then change its color to purple. Can you see a purple ball above your head? If so, change it to every color you can imagine. Then, change it to patterns: polka dots, purple with pink polka dots, black ball with red stripes, etc. Now go back to a white Ping-Pong ball.

Next you have to work on your mental amplifier, your mental zoom lens. Increase the size of the sphere to a baseball. Change the object to softball size. Now to basketball size. Now to a huge ball above your head. You should be able, at will, to change the size of your imagined object to whatever size you would like. Now, whatever sized object you have, split it in half and open the two halves so you can observe the insides. Put the two halves back together. Drill a hole through the object and open it back up. You should be able to observe the through-holes. Once you have gotten to this level of imagineering, there is no stopping. You should be able to see a large pair of dice with all of their numbers in place, and rotate the dice in various directions and see the various numbers.

One hundred percent of the assembly force at Vantec was comprised of women—bored women. When I walked through the assembly area they would all whistle at me and yell funny things. After a while I walked around the building and through a back door when I was too shy to hear their taunts. There was an assembly woman of whom I was fond. I made it a point to stop at her work station and carry on conversations about anything I thought might be of interest to her. One day as I was talking to Peggy, a hornet buzzing around the lights above her flew down and stung her on the back of the neck.

She told me that she was deathly allergic to bee stings and that she did not have her medicine, or anti-venom, with her. I had in my possession one of my syringe inventions connected to a dual check-valve attached to a short length of PVC tubing. I could see where the hornet sting was, so I placed the suction line over the sting and started pumping the auto-return syringe. The clear PVC tubing was easy to see through. The vacuum caused the skin to be drawn up into the tubing from the negative 21 inches of mercury vacuum the syringe could create. Clear liquid bubbled up from the wound as the vacuum worked, removing the poison from her neck. I removed the device and wiped away the fluid. She was fine and went home at the end of the day without a negative allergic reaction.

Three years after that occurrence, after I had left Vantec, I received a call from friends who still worked with Peggy. They informed me that one evening at home after she had dinner with guests, she and her friends took a walk behind her house. A bee stung her and she did not have her medicine with her. By the time they got back to the house she fell into a coma. After a short stay at a local hospital she died. I attended her funeral services. She was so young. How can one little bee kill such a wonderful person as Peggy? I think about that often.

I dated a young lady by the name of Linda. Linda was very good at bowling. She bowled with her right hand. One day she called me at the office and was quite distraught. She said, "I've got a terrible pain in my right hand and I have been to four doctors. None of them can find anything wrong with my hand! I was moving a large cactus plant in my office and a spike jabbed into my hand. I know it's in there but they've taken x-rays and nothing showed up. A different doctor cut the area open and dug around and could find nothing. I've got stitches and it hurts like the dickens." Linda had paid over $250.00 without success.

I told Linda to drive down from Indianapolis to my house after work that evening. I brought a Bausch and Lomb R & D microscope, my auto-syringe, and some silicone tubing home with me that night to see what I could do. That evening she told me, "The last doctor told me that cacti have poison on their tips and that it may be a reaction to the poison." I inspected the stitched area under the inspection scope and could see nothing. There was a little bit of pus where the scalpel had cut through what appeared to be the point of entry. I placed the silicone tubing over her wound and started pumping the syringe. Nothing happened. I placed the tubing over the wound again and pumped up the syringe. Still nothing. Poor Linda was dismayed. She said, "Well, at least you tried." She was very good-natured.

I placed the tubing over the wound one last time and pumped up the device. The wound was sucked up into the tubing but nothing was happening. I told her, "This may hurt a little bit."

She said, "Go for it."

With the suction on full I grasped the tubing and yanked the tubing quickly from her skin. It was incredible. The added suction of pulling the tubing withdrew from the depths of her hand a cactus spike that was almost half an inch long and laid it on her hand. She screamed with disbelief and joy. I told her, "I'll send you the bill." She again bowled with her right hand that week.

Surgical operations are the most incredible thing in the world. The operating team works exactly as that, a TEAM. The best equipment and the strictest procedures are followed over and over again, whether it be in a hospital in California, Michigan, Texas, or Massachusetts. Time and again I was awestruck by the critical importance of what was going on right in front of my eyes. Some patients complain about the cost of medical operations. No one could ever pay me enough to take this kind of responsibility.

During the operations I usually stood directly to the left of the surgeon so I could observe everything that was going on: the procedure, the instruments, and whatever else that was observable. From this vantage point I began to notice, time after time, the faults of medical devices. Many times, a device would break. Other times I could see that the device was almost perfect for the operation but not quite. It might have been much more convenient for the doctor and nurses if only the device were designed like this...or like so....

Many times I did not have an immediate solution for a deficient device. But the inferior device and its faults would stay in my mind. Many times days, weeks, sometimes months afterwards the device problem would nag at my subconscious for a better solution.

I know now where the term "Mad Scientist" comes from. I was waiting in a grocery line for my turn at the cash register. There was no sense in wasting time when I could be working on a safety button for a biopsy device! I saw the device floating above my head; split it open to peer into all the inner mechanics, and observed it operating. It took a long time, but eventually I found a way to jam the trigger with a slide lever so the doctor would not accidentally fire the

device until he was ready for it to be fired. I snapped out of my *imagineering* and noticed that the cash register lady had already rung up
my items and was staring at me with a puzzled expression on her
face as though thinking, "What in the world is wrong with this guy?
What a weirdo! I wonder if he's okay." I turned and noticed that the
line of perhaps six or seven other customers were straining to have
a look at me. The whole line was silent with the same expression on
their faces. I quickly paid her and couldn't get out of there fast
enough. So this is what they mean by mad scientist! I was just lost
in figuring out a very important mechanism on another invention for
Vantec.

It was this kind of focus that led me to introduce over fifty design improvements at Vantec in three years, resulting in four patent
applications with me listed as the inventor.

Starting at the Bottom in the Attic

In 1988 Vantec Inc. was purchased by Boston Scientific Corporation, a minimally invasive surgery company with headquarters located in Boston. When this acquisition occurred in 1988 I decided to resign and start my own medical device company. Usually when you work as an inventor for a company they give you a dollar for each patent. I figured Vantec owed me four dollars and it was this thought that prompted me to strike out on my own.

With the help of my father I began a company in the upstairs of my house. I had earlier added a second story to my house and it stood unfinished inside, a suitable place to build an office and cleanroom for designing and building prototypes for submittal to prospective customers. Our very first sales were to a German medical company, Richard Wolf Medical Instruments Corporation. Wolf's products are pure artistry. My new company, Mectra Labs, Inc., has had a splendid nine-year relationship with the Wolf company and I will always be grateful to them.

We grew very rapidly. In one year we went from one employee, myself, to seventeen. We moved the location of the company to a building in Bloomfield, Indiana. In our line of business, because we ship globally, we do not have customers dropping in on us often so it really doesn't matter where we are located. Bloomfield is a very small community with only a tiny airport and little industry.

The City of Bloomfield welcomed my little company and helped fund the move. One of the advantages start-up companies have in the U.S. is the helpfulness of federal, state, county and city agencies. In the ten years of existence of my company I have never been treated with anything but courtesy and respect by the many government employees with whom I have dealt, including the Food and Drug Administration (FDA). I have never been asked for a bribe or favor. Never. Quite the opposite, their attitude has been, "How can we help *you*?"

About the time we moved Mectra Labs to Bloomfield my wife, Licia, and I agreed that our marriage was at an end. We had such different interests that it was pointless to continue living together. We separated in 1988 and were divorced the next year. This was difficult for both of us but ended a long, painful period of my life. As in many divorces, it was a difficult time for my two daughters. However, they understood the reasons why.

Three years later I met and married a wonderful woman. I met Amy while playing volleyball at the YMCA. The first thing she ever said to me was, "I like your shoes." They were plain white Converse tennis shoes. We have not been apart since. Her family is warm and loving and generous to me. We married on our property one winter in front of a cave in our back woods with our two witnesses, also neighbors, Mike and John. Another friend, Jim, performed the ceremony. Amy and I are like two peas in a pod. We do not argue or fight. We have total respect for one another. We do not try and change one into the other. We appreciate who we've married. One of the many things that drew me to her was her love of animals. We have four cats and a Labrador Retriever, Fergus. He is actually our son trapped in a dog's body and is hooked on phonics as he knows the meaning of at least 100 words since he is home-schooled by her. Now, I am lucky…very lucky…to have a lovely wife, two fine daughters and a great adoptive father and stepmother…plus brothers, sisters, etc. who provide lots of love for me. This is the ultimate healer. Family is best.

Mectra Labs kept growing rapidly even though the medical device field is extremely competitive in the U.S. We grew because we were early in the field of minimally invasive surgery (i.e., belly button surgery). We acquired another customer, a rapidly growing Midwestern distributor. Mectra had a U.S. patent by this time for a medical valve and had several more patents pending. These new products caught on quickly with the Midwestern distributor's customers and our sales through the distributor soon rose to $1,500,000 per year, heady stuff for my two-year-old company. Everything was progressing nicely until we got into a disagreement with the distributor. They insisted on having their medical company name and logo printed on our patented products and they wanted exclusive world distribution rights for our products. We said no! We had expended almost half a million dollars on our patents, molds and trademarks. We were not going to sign them away to a small distributor.

At this point, the Midwestern distributor did something that I had not experienced before, nor have I since: they set up an alternative source for our products, placed a large order for our products and then abruptly cancelled the order, leaving us with a huge inventory of parts. Furthermore, they delayed paying us for products we had already shipped. This left us in perilous financial shape which might have been their intention. We managed to get paid in three months for the products we had shipped by appealing to a national credit rating agency. However, it took over three years to use up the inventory of parts left over from this fiasco. Happily, this was a unique experience. I have found that other customers and suppliers are highly professional in dealing with us. As with government employees, I have never been asked for nor given a bribe by another business representative. This is another American strength. I know there is some dishonesty in business and government but I think it is the exception.

The Midwestern distributor who caused us the difficulty did not go unscathed. Their second source did not know all the intricacies of building our products. The substitute products physically fell apart in surgery. They also ran into a multitude of other problems. The president of the Midwestern distributor, after a three- to four-month period, called me to ask for more Mectra products. I answered him that I would never, ever in my life sell anything to him again. "He who laughs last...."

We had 68 employees when we were cut off abruptly by the distributor. We had to lay off more than half of them immediately to survive. Gone were our plans to provide lifetime employment for our workers. We were in a "crash mode." We moved our R&D and Administrative operations out of a first-class building to a window-less 6,000-square-foot shed made of corrugated metal. We then acquired a data base of all the hospitals in the U.S. and began shipping Mectra products directly to the users. Our sales, once again, began to rise.

By using a satellite TV antenna I have long been able to view surgeries at home. By this means and by visiting hospital surgery rooms, I observed over 2,000 surgeries from California to Massachusetts over a period of 14 years. I have also seen, touched, and analyzed under an inspection microscope, over 5,000 different medical devices. All this exposure to medical procedures and devices has given me a stimulus to invent many products. Most of them are quite simple. Being president of a small company mandates that product designs be simple. Money for tooling is limited so simplicity is a must. Every additional part in a product means more tooling, more cost.

At the present time I have 20 U.S. patents issued in my name for Mectra Labs and have three pending. Patents are very expensive to get and we have not received the patent royalties that we once envisioned. But having a patent portfolio means that we won't be blindsided by someone else's patents and forced to withdraw some of our products from the marketplace after spending precious resources to develop and market them. We still sell through distributors and our having patents gives them comfort also.

In 1993 we retained a venture capital firm, Hambrecht & Quist, to evaluate our company and recommend among a number of options, including being partially or entirely acquired by another company. Out of the evaluation came the recommendation that we seek to be acquired because, in their words, "The Clinton plan to consolidate the health care industry will cause the large corporations currently serving the market to act in the near future *like stampeding elephants.*" Their message was clear: you are a mouse and you are about to get stepped on.

As it turned out we elected not to be acquired and we have been *running with the elephants.* Actually, I cannot point to a single instance where an elephant has intentionally stepped on us. But it is the nature of elephants to focus on other elephants in a stampede and mice have to try to avoid the large feet themselves. We have had many sleepless nights during the past five years worrying about a shortage of orders one week, too many to supply the next. Always, there is the fear of the unknown: suppose, just suppose, X does this or Y fails to do that. The margin for survival for a start-up company is sometimes perilously thin.

In time we built a relationship with the Ethicon Division of Johnson & Johnson Corporation as a supplier to them. This has been a great boon to us since they are on the leading edge of technology in the field of surgical devices.

On the plus side, working for one's self can be very rewarding. I worked for large companies and am familiar with the infighting that sometimes occurs, and the steady movement of managers that places employees in a constant state of uneasiness. Recently, I have been exposed to large corporation executives who exhibit signs of stress from jetting from continent to continent. I work very hard and haven't had a vacation in five years. But I don't think I am nearly as stressed as some of the executives I meet from other companies who have broader product responsibilities spread over a larger geographic area.

At Mectra Labs we are aided by computers, the Internet, TV conferencing and many other telecommunication advances. This enables us to monitor what our competitors are doing to a degree, but only to a degree. I am struck by the advances that have been made in medical products since I started in this business 14 years ago, and by the acceleration in the rate of advance. Somebody once said, "The rich should learn how the poor live and the poor how the rich work." I am certainly not rich, although I hope to be someday. But if you substitute *business executive* for the word *rich* in the above statement, it really resonates for me now. Too often business executives get a bad rap in the U.S. media. Operating within the freest trade policies in the world, U.S. business executives, particularly those engaged in the manufacturing sector, are under tremendous pressure to perform day after day after day at an accelerating pace. Most of us love it but the pressure is tremendous.

Every year the Medical Device Manufacturers Association holds a trade show to give companies an opportunity to display their ware to customers. One year I flew myself and several other Mectra Labs employees to New York to attend this show because we were in need of a lot of components.

One evening while there we all went "clubbing." On the way back to the hotel, we were walking along a poorly lit street when a very athletic looking guy walked toward us until he got to me. I was the last in our line walking along the sidewalk. He hit me in the shoulder with his elbow. When he did this, he let his drink fall to the ground and made believe that the *joint* in his hand was jolted forwards out of control.

He turned and came right at me. He said, "Don't yell for the police or I'll hit you as hard as I can and run into the darkness and they'll never catch me."

I thought, "Oh man...I'm so tired. I don't want to knock out this poor street guy. We're in trouble." My employees did not see what had happened. Keeping my eye on this guy at all times so as not to get sucker punched, I told everyone, "Walk toward those lights up there behind that building."

We all walked toward the lights which were toward the back of a hotel. The stranger stayed right with me. I could tell that he was looking for an opportunity to sucker-punch me. He said, "You hit me in my arm, made me spill my drink, and lose the joint that I was rolling. You owe me five bucks."

I answered, "Hey man, you're trippin'. I'm not giving you five bucks. This is your gig. You go up to people and terrorize them until they give you money to go away. I'm not giving you anything."

He would not go away. He followed us over to the back of the lit building insisting on five bucks or he was going to fight me. I kept telling him over and over I wasn't going to fight him and I wasn't going to give him five bucks. When we got into the lights, I said, "This is the way you make a living, terrorizing people and I'm not going to give you any money for that."

He answered, "Hey man, I'm an architect. You made me lose five bucks. You owe me."

It looked like I was not going to get out of this one without a fight. Many times in the past I had gladly fought. But this time it was different. I felt sorry for this guy. He was a street person. I used to be a street person. I didn't want to hurt him. I figured I could easily knock him out so I told him, "Some day, you're going to meet up with someone who is going to hurt you badly."

I squatted down to the ground and stood up to feel which pair of pants I had on. I owned two kinds of denim pants but I didn't want to take my eyes off him to look down to see which pants I had on. One pair is by Levi's and is like wearing a straightjacket; there is no room for movement. The others were stretch denims; I could do splits with them on. They look like the others, but are as elastic as a rubber band. To my relief, I had my stretch denims on.

A woman security guard from the hotel saw everything happening and sized up the situation accurately. She came over and grabbed my elbow saying, "Sir, you should come into the hotel lobby."

"No, actually, we would like a taxi," I replied. She must have had her transmitter on because I had no sooner said that when a taxi drove up and its doors flew open. Relieved, we piled into the car and drove away without incident.

The next day, one of my employees kept saying over and over, "Why didn't you knock him out? You could have kicked him in the head. Why didn't you do it?"

I thought for a while and answered, "That poor guy is a street person. That is the way he makes his living; I felt sorry for him. It's like if you came to work at Mectra Labs one day and someone knocked you out."

He looked a little bewildered, "Do you think you could have beat him?"

"No doubt," I answered, " I've knocked down people a lot taller and stronger than he. But what's the point? If he had asked for money nicely, I would have gladly given him some. If he had taken the first swing at me, I would have knocked him out." My family was very unhappy when they heard about this incident. They had heard of people being shot or stabbed under similar circumstances.

Demons

Sometimes the pressures of family and business get to me. Sometimes the doubts come back: Am I a worthy person? Am I a capable person? Am I a truly good person? I suppose everybody has periods like this. For an orphan these periods of self-doubt are heightened by unanswerable questions: Who am I? Who were my family? Who are my family? I call these times of self-examination *my demons*.

Work helps when the demons arrive. I can usually bury myself in day-to-day problems of running a business. That is until exhaustion takes over. I can lie awake at night just so many nights before I begin to unravel. I can sometimes find relief by physical work. I am the greatest rock carrier in the nation. Amy and I were lucky enough to buy 50 acres of land covered by trees and rocks together with a house, barn and small guesthouse. This gives me lots of opportunity to work off demons. I have built rock walls, rock gardens, paths, steps and fountains. If the demons persist I will turn the entire property into a rock castle.

One of the greatest joys for us is to entertain friends at our home. Jo Kang, a journalism student, and her parents visited. Jo's parents had come from Korea to visit her. One of my dearest friends, Pearl, brought some small girls whom she mentors in Chicago to spend a weekend. Pearl is a prime example of someone who gives of herself for the benefit of others. The girls were from Laos, Vietnam and Cambodia. Each of them was incredibly beautiful. They loved catching frogs and riding our four-wheeler around the woods and fields.

For me, many things in life can be boiled down to the Yin and Yang. After experiencing the joy of Pearl and her friends, I became very angry at the world. How can we drop bombs on people, let alone children? Many times I hear the question, "What is the meaning of life?" What if we all did what Pearl does? I think she is closer to the meaning of life than most. What if we all decided the meaning was to help others? Could you imagine what this world would be like if every single individual took up as their personal mission to help others?

Amy, Fergus and Thomas

Of all the countries on earth, America seems to me to be the most dedicated to helping others. Americans expend a huge amount of time, money, lives, and effort to help others not as fortunate. I am a living example of this. I hate war and fighting. But it is the Yin and Yang once again. Do I suggest dismantling our military? Not on your life! How can I who was born in a war, who hates war, want a strong military? Yin and Yang.

I wish by the year 2000 all countries would decide to play a war game with new rules. They would be this: No more battles where people live. Instead, there would be a designated island where the two opposing factions would meet. They would not use conventional weapons. They would not wear clothes. All they would be equipped with are Styrofoam bowls of mashed potatoes which they would relentlessly fling at each other. After the mashed potato war the two sides would sit down and feed each other, wipe food from each other's eyes, and become the best of friends.

The LA riots bothered me very much because people of color fought with the Korean-Americans. Fighting in general bothers me. Fighting black on yellow is even worse. Koreans have gone through the same prejudices as the blacks everywhere in the world. I used to go to nightclubs with some "sisters and brothers." I would be the only non-black person there. It never bothered me because I was accustomed to being the only Korean in many social events. They were always amazed when they came to my house because I had many rap and hip-hop dance tapes. Rock and roll music is very difficult to dance to. There is no "heartbeat" in it. How does one dance to music with no heartbeat?

I think about other species on our planet. Let's think about fruit trees. They are such a symbolic representation of so many things in life. They grow from little seeds. With the correct light and nourishment, they grow into large trees like their parents, so that one day they too may bear fruit. Scientists know that many plants and trees can not survive in all environments. If you take an orange tree seedling and plant it in Canada, perhaps it will grow slowly in the summer but when winter comes, it will die. The environment is too harsh. All plants are not genetically engineered to grow and bear fruit in all climates. However, scientists engineer various strains of the fruit tree by grafting and cross-pollinating a new breed, a new strain which can not only bear delicious fruit but also withstand a much harsher environment than a purebred fruit tree. Need I say more? A half-and-half like me is a genetic hybrid! We are not purebred...we are hybrid...able to survive and flourish in a dynamic world economy.

To relieve some of the stress which comes with the territory of executive life in a fast-moving field, I took up a hobby, trapezing. Trapeze, now there's a safe sport. If the equipment is not 100%, it can be a pain in the neck. Bernadette Pace, who owns a trapeze rig in Bloomington, is very generous with her time. She is very patient. She coaches everyone to be either a *catcher* or a *flyer*. I was trained by her to be a catcher. We worked with a trapeze 32 feet off the ground so, even with a net, we were always at risk of injury. I think that is why it appealed to me. I like to push the envelope. I don't want to get hurt, mind you, but I like the risk.

This is a sport where practice and timing are everything. We had many professional flyers from all over the world stop by at our trapeze facility to practice. We amateurs performed at local functions. Sometimes we were paid and sometimes we donated our time. We performed at a "Just Say No To Drugs" benefit in Indianapolis. NBC-TV came and filmed our group in practice and at a performance. It was very exciting to be filmed by a national network. I got to catch the Luna brothers, who are known for being able to do a quad. A quad means instead of doing a single flip prior to being caught, you do four flips before coming out of the spin to get caught.

One year, my *High Flyers* trapeze group pooled their money and went to Belize in the Caribbean for a two-week scuba diving vacation. The ocean life there is out of this world. My hotel roommate, George, went up to an incandescent, six-foot long, urn-shaped fungus which was glowing an eerie blue color. When he looked inside, a huge fish, every bit as large as the fungus, shot straight up from it, scaring the heck out of both of us.

One day our crew went out several miles from the shore. When scuba diving, it is a good policy for everyone to stick together. We were diving at around 80 feet when from out of nowhere an under-

Hanging out at the bars

water dust storm blew in, obscuring our vision to less than one foot. Bernadette, who was with me at the time, and I became separated from the rest of the group. She did the sensible thing, which was to surface. I did the ignorant thing, which was to turn back and look for the group. I was swimming with the flow of the dust current. It appeared to me as though I was swimming horizontally. It wasn't until I had to decompress my mask a few times that I checked my

Doing a one and a half

depth gauge and noticed I was now at around 130 feet! I had been swimming vertically instead of horizontally.

When you are at those depths you can't just swim up to the surface or you will get what is called the bends. I followed my bubbles as they rose and had to stop and wait for a period of time. There was no one around. Thoughts of a possible shark attack gave me moments of panic but I suppressed them. I swam up a little further and waited again. I was all alone in the dark. Eventually I surfaced, but it took a while.

Clowning around

By the time I reached the surface the boat was nowhere to be seen. Ocean currents had moved it far into the distance. Apparently, they all thought that this was the last time they would ever see me again. My roommate, George, had thoughts of sadly packing my stuff for the journey back to the U.S. I finally spotted them. They were a little tiny speck way off in the distance; they were searching for me. I waved my arms back and forth and Beth, a woman I trapezed with, saw me and drew them back to my rescue. It was a very close call.

When scuba diving, if separated from the group, you should never go searching. You should always *surface* immediately. This might sound like an inane analogy, but sometimes as an international adoptee, I feel very isolated and alone. I think it would be good for any adoptee who feels like this to *surface*. By *surface*, I mean get connected to an organization of similar adoptees. For example, a relevant group may be located through an internet search, public libraries, or phone books. There is no sense floating around lost waiting for a shark attack when all you need to do is *surface*, wave your arms and say, "Over here!"

If you ever get a chance to see a trapeze group perform *live*, you should. It's simply amazing. These people are risking life and limb for your entertainment. I had a young friend who fell from 28 feet without a safety net. Fortunately she not only lived but she is back flying to this very day. I used to catch my daughters, Jessica and Jennifer, with a net of course. Eventually, Mectra Labs required so much attention that I had to quit this time-consuming sport and concentrate on business.

Spiritual Cousins

Mectra Labs, Inc. has a web site: http://www.mectralabs.com. I was surfing the web one day and wondered if I were to go into a search engine would I find anything listed under *Korean Adoptee*. After typing in the key search words many hits came up on the screen. I had hundreds of choices. I picked one which was made by a journalist, Crystal Chappell, also a Korean/American adoptee.

It was the most incredible feeling in the world. After 40 years of being in the United States it occurred to me that I hadn't ever known or seen or met another KAA. I was not the only Korean adoptee in the U.S. after all! I sent her an e-mail from my computer, so she called me for a telephone interview. In the interview I confided, "I have many things in life: a sports car, house, guitars, a wonderful wife, children, good health, my own company, everything that anyone could ever hope to have. But there is something missing way deep down inside of me. It's like there is intangible, unfinished business, a sadness in my heart. I can't put my finger on it, but it is definitely there. I wonder if any other adoptees have this feeling." We have been fast friends ever since. We are brother and sister to each other.

She told me that I should attend a meeting in LA called the GKN-LA Winter Conference. This was the very first time that Korean/American adoptees had been formally invited by a Korean-run organization to join them in a conference. GKN is the acronym for Global Korean Network. I was very excited about attending due to the fact that this would be my first time meeting other adoptees. Through the web I had discovered a whole community of cyber Korean adoptees.

The strange thing was that because the web is global, my new friends were scattered all across the world from Australia, Europe, Korea, Africa, Canada, and all over the U.S. After communicating with an adoptee who lived in Australia, I told him, "You sound just like an Aussie."

He replied, "I *am* an Aussie." Yes, if you were born in Korea and lived in Australia, you would be an Aussie. If you lived in Germany, you would be German. If you lived in the U.S.A., you would be an American.

I attended the LA meeting. The first night there, which was a Thursday, we met at Jo Rankin's house so that I could ease into meeting a dozen or so adoptees. Suzanne, a very energetic adoptee who appeared to know everyone and anyone, asked me, "Now that you've met your very first Korean/American adoptees, what do you think?"

I answered, "It's very strange! First of all, I've talked to you on the phone and communicated with many via computer and I talk to you all here right now. I must say, you all sound *very* American. However, you all *look* very Korean. It is a weird thing."

Suzanne laughed. We all had pizza and got things organized for the adoptee meeting. Suzanne said, "Should we all get started?" As soon as she said this, out of nowhere a multitude of notebook computers, electronic note pads, modem connectors and cellular phones appeared. Wow, this group of Korean/American adoptees was highly technical and well prepared!

The next day six of us went to an LA radio station for an hour interview. The radio interviewer was so interested in what we had to say that the interview went on for three hours. It was very nice that after 40 years of silence, the ice had been broken. The interviewer ended by saying something to the effect that we all seemed very well-adjusted and happy. We were and are. We all left the station and headed back to the Korean hotel to greet the rest of the 65 KAA's flying in from all over the country plus a social worker from Korea.

Friday evening there was a meeting for just the adoptees. The meeting started with representatives from various adoptee groups talking about their respective organizations, followed by each adoptee getting up in front of the group to tell a little about themselves: where they were born, how old they were when adopted (if they knew), where they lived, and anything else they would like to say to the group. It was a highly emotional thing for me. I am very used to talking in front of people about technical things. When it comes to personal things like the Korean War, living on the streets, living in an orphanage, integrating into the American society, it is a different story. I could barely keep from getting very emotional.

A friend, Eric, later told me that what I must do is practice. Practice will harden yourself so that you can get your message out without falling apart. I have been practicing, but emotions still have a way of creeping up on me. It is all that I can do to get them under control and continue with whatever I am saying. Perhaps I shouldn't worry about it. It just shows I'm human.

The conference started on Saturday. I had volunteered to be a panelist. It seemed easy enough when I volunteered. However, I was now seated on a stage in front of an audience with microphones and a center podium where Suzanne, the panel discussion leader, stood. I had written so many notes and messages on my script prior to the meeting that I could no longer make heads or tails of anything that I had jotted down. So on a blank piece of paper, I drew five large black lines across with a magic marker and made large musical notes in hopes that I could focus on these musical notes if I got too nervous.

Once up in front of the audience, doubts began to creep in. Looking across the audience I noticed how beautiful all these Korean people were! I thought to myself, "Why in the world did I volunteer to be on the panel! This is horrifying! I just want to go back to my seat and say, 'I'm sorry, I just can't do this,'" And then it happened. My attention went to Suzanne, who had apparently asked me a question and ended it with "Mr. Clement." I had no idea what she had just asked me. I held up the musical notes so that everyone could see and said, "I brought my notes but they aren't very useful to me. I'm sorry, would you please repeat the question?" The audience laughed at my notes, which helped ease the tension a great deal. I still had a hard time speaking because the focus was on Korea and myself. Someday perhaps I will be able to talk about my past without having so much difficulty. Maybe I will always have difficulty.

To close the panel discussion, each of us was to deliver a message to the group. My message was, "If I think about the Korean War, living on the streets and the orphanage, I could be 'totaled' by these thoughts; or I can use these life experiences to *feed the fire...feed the fire* to motivate me to make a positive change...make

the world a better place for our children in the future." This attitude
I owe to my parents.

One of the attendees at the conference read the old newspaper
article about Mika and me arriving at the airport and wanted to know
if I had ever talked to her since our arrival. Not only had I not spoken with her since, I had no idea where she was living. It took two
weeks to locate her. The next thing I knew, I was on the phone talking with someone who connected my past to the present. So it
wasn't a dream after all!

We talked about Korea and the orphanage. She told me that one
day she was next to the pond where the dam was and fell into the
water. A lady dove in and saved her. I couldn't believe it! I was
there! She gave me a piece of chewing gum on the airplane and I had
not seen her since. After we walked down the stairs from the plane
and were holding onto our new parents, I had my right hand behind
my back holding onto her dress as tightly as I could. Mika said that
she hated the huge glass windows at the orphanage because at night
we faced them when we slept. The sky was dark and ominous at
night. One night the air raid sirens blared so the lights were turned
off. The kids all began to scream. We were all huddled next to a wall
as instructed by the counselors. It is much safer next to walls in the
event of a roof collapse. I looked through the huge windows to
watch a bomb explode but could not see anything. We heard
whistling noises and explosions. We thought the war monster had
come back. This occurred after the cease fire in 1953. Possibly we
mistook South Korean military exercises for the real thing. I hated
the sound of screaming children more than the sound of the explosions. I hated those huge windows too.

One day I hope to go back to my motherland, Korea. I want to
plant my feet on the soil, walk around and see the country, and meet
the people who I left long ago. I would like to do many things there.
Who knows...some day I may even meet my birth mother. I would
tell her I have missed her throughout these years and have thought
of her.

It's odd that I don't have a burning desire to find her. It may be
that the magnitude of the love which my adoptive mother and father
gave me through the years has overshadowed the loss of my birth

mother and the desire to find her. It could be that the task of the search is so overwhelming, along with the fact that if she has remarried, I am sure the new family knows nothing of my existence. And the fact that half-and-half Koreans are still looked down upon diminishes my curiosity to a low hum in my heart which says, "Don't set yourself up for a disappointment, Thomas. If she didn't want you then, what makes you think she'd want you now?"

I am also very apprehensive about visiting Korea because I fear the second I get off the plane the war will begin again. I have ghosts which still visit me from time to time...the flashing of bombs, the booming sounds of their explosions, gunfire, and people screaming. Will they ever go away and let me rest in peace? Probably not.

Message to Adoptive Parents

First a word for prospective parents of a foreign orphan: adopted foreign children are children plus. That is, you should expect all the joys and frustrations of raising your own child plus the problems of guiding a child through the shoals of possible racial and cultural differences. As with any adoptee, the foreign adoptee brings memories of the past, including possible abuse. All in all, therefore, foreign orphans brings with them the prospect of very eventful childhoods in their new home and land.

Because foreign adoptees are children plus, it is important that the adopting parents be stable, mature adults. Raising a foreign child is a very slender reed to be used for support of unstable adults in an unstable marriage. Adopted children need continued reassurance that they are loved by both parents and that life in the new home will be permanent. Time, lots of time, will be needed for the adoptees to gain confidence in their new surroundings. A child is not a hothouse plant that can be forced to maturity. Time does not heal all things, but it is a great healer. Don't try to push your adopted child into early resolution of his or her problems. You may want yourself to seek counseling regarding aspects of your child's behavior. But probing the psyche of the child may open a Pandora's box.

For those who have already adopted, thank you for having it in your heart to adopt a foreign child. If you have been blessed with the adoption of an international child, from the very beginning always make a conscious effort to educate yourself and your new family member about the cultural background from which the child has come. Keeping articles around the house from the birth country is a good physical reminder that speaks louder than words. Food, chopsticks, clothing, a flag, pictures, books and even furniture are a few things which would be very good to have in your household.

Disclose from the beginning that he or she was adopted. Use a map or globe to show the birth country and the current location. Videotapes on the other culture are excellent. There are many cultural camps specifically designed for foreign-born adopted children so that they may be around others who look similar to them. Such camps are scattered across the U.S. It is very important for adopted children to associate with other adoptees so that they know they are not an oddity.

Adoptive parents should be supportive if their young adult wants to search for birth parents. It does not mean that your adopted child loves you any less. This is a very personal mission and should be supported with a positive attitude. After graduating from high school or college, it may be a good idea for the adoptee to visit the birth country and meet the people there. Learning how to speak at least some of the language of the birth country is also an excellent idea. If you are the parent of a Korean child and have the need to acquire more information pertaining to this subject, I suggest that you contact one of the national organizations that deal with Korean adoptee affairs.

The best support a parent may give a child beginning a birth parent search is to help prepare for possible disappointment. Many searches do not result in success. Some birth mothers have passed away, while others do not want the fact known they had an illegitimate child. Deception can also play a role in the search process. A searching adoptee may find numerous "birth parents" eagerly insisting they are indeed the actual parent if it becomes known that the searcher is living in America and is affluent. The language barrier can also pose a problem. What if you find your birth mother; she doesn't speak English; and you don't speak her language?

Another problem: in some countries, half-and-half orphans are not allowed to obtain citizenship. They have no political voting rights, nor are they allowed an education or equal employment. Here in America, I have all those rights and privileges. I have three college degrees and am the President/CEO of a medical device company whose products have touched the lives of millions of Americans. If my life story says and does anything, I hope that it helps change the political and social attitude some countries have toward a most valuable, untapped resource, the half-and-half orphans, and orphans in general.

Although education played a huge role in where I am today, it was not the single most important factor. The most important influence was the love and support I received from my adoptive parents and family. Actions speak louder than words; always have and always will. Throughout my life in America, my father always said to me, "Tom, try to be the very best you can be; do that and we will support you 100 percent." It was the knowledge of this kind of commitment from my adoptive family that has allowed me to flourish as a human being.

The Lottery

What am I to make of my life so far? What have I learned?

I have learned that happiness is in the doing. There is no permanent state of being called happiness. Happiness is often found like a jewel in the strangest places. It is found by both the rich and the poor, sometimes even more by the poor. Happiness is, above all, about achievement.

I have learned that, in a purely biological sense, we are all programmed to sustain our own species. Put simply, biologically we are all about propagating our DNA. This insight leads me to conclude that prejudice is natural, inevitable and universal. We all instinctively prefer our own kind because we sense that this is the best strategy for our species to live and prosper.

Prejudice is not just about race and religion. Who can say that they are not prejudiced in some way: against people whom they feel are too fat or too thin, too conservative or too liberal, too timid or too bold, too sophisticated or too gauche, too Northern or too Southern? And who has not been subjected to prejudice by others?

I have found that prejudice can best be overcome by individuals and groups who meet with prejudice by excelling in things that are universally prized by humankind: love of family, education, hard work, civility and charity. Instead of succumbing to a feeling of victimhood, those who experience the pain of prejudice ought to dedicate themselves to the pursuit of excellence with the conviction that all else is unimportant. "Sticks and stones..." Prejudice demeans the perpetrator, not the recipient. Move on!

I don't deny that government has a responsibility for helping lessen prejudice through laws and education. It is just that my observation of the advances made by some minorities, Asian Americans for example, in erasing long-held American prejudices against them, leads me to conclude that salvation comes most quickly and surely through one's own effort. That is, by excelling in things most admired by all humankind.

It is important to excel not only for one's self. Each of us has an obligation to many others: to family, country, race, religion and humankind in general. When I moved to America I wanted to be like other Americans. I was proud of my new country and my new family. I wanted to be a contributor to both. I rejected my adoptive parents' early effort to provide me with contact with my native land. As a result of my treatment in Korea I thought I did not want to be Korean. But, unknown to me and my parents, I secretly wanted to identify with the land of my birth. As I approached adulthood I discovered that I was proud of my native land and her people. I secretly thrilled at reports of the success of the Korean people in their struggle to rebuild their economy after the war and to join the industrialized world. You might say that this new-found pride was part of my biological imperative, to want to see my species thrive. Today I watch KBS (The Korean Broadcasting System) regularly on television in order to learn about Korea and pick up some Korean words. I now have Korean friends in America and feel very much at ease with them and they with me. I am American and I am Korean, and better off for being both.

I view myself as a potential global bridge between Korea and America. What better bridge can there be than an individual who is the product of two different societies…half and half…half Korean and half American in my case.

In my life so far I have also learned that I can always take one more step. Even when reason argued that it made no sense to try, that it was hopeless…I have found that I *could* take one more step, and then another. My life has become a journey punctuated by terrors, doubts and, at times, a sense of utter hopelessness. But I have found that I can always go on. My advice to people who feel lost is: *take one more step*.

Last year at the symposium in Los Angeles I was asked, "Why are you so full of smiles, so positive? You have suffered terrible hardships; you have been spat at, called 'roundeye' in Korea and 'slanteye' in America. Why aren't you bitter?"

I replied, completely spontaneously, "I won the lottery." I did, in a sense, win the lottery, the lottery called life. True, I have been spat at but I had a birth mother and her family who loved and protected me through the critical first four or five years of my life. This gave me an essential confidence in people so that I mostly look for good in others and dismiss instances of hate as aberrations. True, I have been called "roundeye" in Korea and "slanteye" in America, but I have grown to adulthood with what some people consider an exotic appearance, a not unattractive one. Why should I complain? I have been cast out but I have been reclaimed. I have been knocked down by some but picked up by others. I still have nightmares and I still see demons. But I can say with confidence to other troubled people, "I can make it and you can too!"

As for the rest of my life, I see many rewarding experiences for me ahead, talking to young Americans, some of them adoptees like me, about the promise of America and the world...urging them to hold on, to suffer their demons and still have faith in the inherent goodness of people in spite of the hate and prejudice that sometimes mar their lives.

On Being Adopted

By Kim Maher

Little one, who cares for you?
Your mother and your father care
Who is my mother?
Who is my father?
The womb that held me?
Or the arms that hold me?
The man that made me?
Or the heart that molds me?
Both, my child, both
The ones who gave you life
And the ones who give you life
The ones who bore you
And the ones who adore you
Don't shame either